The Wiles of the Devil

Using the whole armour of God

Dennesha K Frazer

WestBow
PRESS
A DIVISION OF THOMAS NELSON

WestBow Press books may be ordered through booksellers or by contacting:

WestBow Press
A Division of Thomas Nelson
1663 Liberty Drive
Bloomington, IN 47403
www.westbowpress.com
1-(866) 928-1240

Because of the dynamic nature of the Internet, any web addresses or links contained in this book may have changed since publication and may no longer be valid. The views expressed in this work are solely those of the author and do not necessarily reflect the views of the publisher, and the publisher hereby disclaims any responsibility for them.

Any people depicted in stock imagery provided by Thinkstock are models, and such images are being used for illustrative purposes only.

Certain stock imagery © Thinkstock.

ISBN: 978-1-4497-2864-9 (sc)
ISBN: 978-1-4497-2865-6 (dj)
ISBN: 978-1-4497-2863-2 (e)

Library of Congress Control Number: 2011918051

Printed in the United States of America

WestBow Press rev. date: 10/19/2011

To God

I dedicate this book to God and the calling he has placed upon my life. I receive the calling to share what he has to say to me with all his wonderful children. As a sign of my commitment to this call, I offer my time, resources and effort in writing whatever he bids me to. I arise to the birthing of a Ministry in writing; I answer the call of God and give him back that which he has given to me as a tool to comfort his loved and his own. I dedicate this work to the Almighty God.

Acknowledgement

I would like to acknowledge the persons who have aided in the preparation and completion of this work. Without the assistance of these dear ones I would not have been able to successfully accomplish this task.

I would like to first acknowledge Bishop Carlton Facey of the Greater Highway Redemption Ministries in Toronto Canada whose prophetic voice confirmed to me the call of God upon my life to write this book. Secondly, I hasten to thank Pastor Cargill Barrett who encouraged me through the early stages of writing. Thanks to Mrs. Pauleen Reid who did the final editing of my manuscript and who edged me on to complete this task.

I am most grateful to my mother Jennivieve Campbell Clarke for her financial support and her continued love. My best friend and Sister Joseth Ann- Marie Kerr must also be acknowledged for her confidence in my abilities and her high expectations which propelled me every step of the way. I am also eternally grateful to my church mother Missionary Sandria Chung- Kerr for her continued prayers and encouragements.

Finally, God must be praised for He has been a keeper, a provider and a caring and loving father.

Contents

Forward

"This book is a refreshing reminder" Pastor C. Barrett

"This is a great book which stirs the Christian to take action and do right." Missionary Joseth A. Kerr M.Sc. B.ed. DIP.

"Perfect piece of writing. This is a book of wisdom" Former Lecturer Dahla Fuller MSc. Bsc. DIP.

Preface

This book is written to intensify Christian ministry, advance evangelism and empower those who are bombarded by the tricks of the enemy.

For the better part of six thousand years, the Devil has run unchecked or rather unstudied; damaging thousands of lives by using the same devices, repeatedly. Now the time has come when his master tricks in his book of devices will be brought to the fore.

The battle is most definitely in the mind but the mind needs some equipping. A mighty man loses all battles if he is unable to recognize his enemy. The secret of Satan is in his devices. No wonder the apostle Paul implored the Corinthian brethren not to be ignorant of the Devil's devices. King James Version (II Corinthians 2:11).

A **wile**, as it is used in the scriptures, is a plan, a trick or a strategy to overtake. All the Devil has ever wanted to do from the beginning and still wants to do is to take over or get dominion of humanity. The Devil, having had many years of experience, reuses the **wiles** that have been most effective. He has used the same **wile**s in different ways hoping to get the same result of- victory for himself. As believers in Jesus Christ, we need to know how the enemy will come at us- at what time and through whom.

This book with its scope of readers spanning all the age groups will fortify for Spiritual warfare. The battle is the Lord's but you need to know what battle you are in. If a soldier does not know his enemies then he can lose the simplest battle even though he has the best artillery.

Let me not fail to point out that the only way to overcome a **wile** of Satan is to identify the root cause behind that **wile** and attack it through the power of the anointing. The yoke breaking anointing that is upon the Spirit filled believer, provides a dynamite power to overcome all things. It is in killing the root that you will overcome or destroy the shoot.

This book features some of the most used **wiles** and offers insight into the root causes of each **wile**. There is also knowledge provided on how to kill each root by a practical Spiritual application.

Those tender years of being a new convert, the hunger to know all there is to know about Christ, the falls and restarts, the lukewarm state, the teenage years, the middle aged crisis of finding a partner for marriage, the balancing act of family and a relationship with Christ and so many other stages too many to mention, are experienced by most of us. Each stage has its own challenges. I therefore thank God for the Word, for experienced saints, for personal experiences and especially for the Spirits of Counsel and wisdom which all have equipped me to come to your assistance.

Benefits

This book is of great value whether or not you are in in a relationship with the Lord and Saviour Jesus Christ because it will evoke in you the awareness of the enemy's wiles and will give rise to a deep desire to know Christ and his resurrected power so as to avoid any entrapment by Satan.

Through internalizing the contents of this book, you will be well able to recognize the enemy from a far off. This will give you the opportunity to plan your moves ahead of time. You will always be one step ahead of the enemy. Knowledge will prevent you from being destroyed. You will become knowledgeable about the **wile**s of Satan, what makes you vulnerable to them and how to counteract them. BE IN THE KNOW.

Know 'The **Wile**s of the Devil'

Introduction

What is a Wile?

A Bible commentary I came across some years ago puts it perfectly:

"The word rendered '**wile**s' meyodeia means, properly, that which is traced out with method; that which is methodized; and then that which is well laid—art, skill, and cunning". It means cunning devices, arts, attempts to delude and destroy us. It said that the **wile**s of the Devil are the various arts and stratagems which he employs to drag souls down to perdition. "Satan does not carry on an open warfare", the article goes on to postulate. He does not meet the Christian soldier face to face. He advances covertly; makes his approaches in darkness; employs cunning rather than power, and seeks rather to deceive and betray than to vanquish by mere force. Hence the necessity of being constantly armed to meet him whenever the attack is made.

The commentary went on to say things such as: "a man who has to contend with a visible enemy may feel safe, if he only prepares to meet him in the open field. But far different is the case if the enemy is invisible; if he steals upon us slyly and stealthily; if he practises war only by ambushes and by surprises". Such is the foe with which we have to contend and almost all the Christian struggle is warfare against stratagems and **wile**s. "Satan does not openly appear. He approaches us not in repulsive forms, but comes to recommend some plausible doctrine, to lay before us some temptation that does not immediately repel us. He presents the world in an alluring aspect; invites to pleasures that seem to be harmless; and leads us in indulgence, until we have gone too far to retreat."

This is an interesting discourse. It deals with **wiles** in the very way that this book will tackle them; as traps intertwined into the dainties of life. Of course the Devil would not show up in a black or a red suit with a flaming fork, to take you out for lunch. For who then would go with him? Therefore, he chooses our routine, that which we like and that with which we are familiar. He also plays on our weaknesses since he knows them very well. Let me pause to ask a question: Has the Devil ever tempted you with something that you didn't care for? Or could he? Your answer being no, we proceed into the study of his devices.

Table of Wiles

---

1   (Frazer, 2008) Wiles are not organized in any particular order.

Chapter One

The wile of Procrastination

Have you ever had a plan to do a certain Spiritual task on a regular basis? Perhaps this task was praying or reading the Bible. Then, after doing it two or three or even four times, you found yourself putting it off until you were off to an irregular pattern and were inconsistent.

Has the Lord ever moved you to witness to someone or correct someone, and you put it off until you never got it done? Well, this is the story of many. The unscrupulous enemy has something to do with this. Let me share a story with you which will put this matter into perspective.

Anecdote

A friend of mine once shared an experience that will stay with me for the rest of my life.

While this friend walked in a busy town one afternoon, he paced passed a certain corner, and there stood a woman who caught his eyes. Something went off in his Spirit. The Spirit of God immediately bade him to go over and share the gospel message with her. At that very instant, he started to assess her by her appearance. *Hard, unreachable and not likely to respond to the gospel* were some of the evaluating terms that flooded his mind. He therefore disobeyed the Spirit's leading and walked on by the woman. His conscience worried him and gnawed at him for quite a while. Instead of turning back immediately and witnessing to this woman,

1

he promised himself and the Spirit that he would return to that street a few minutes later to do the job. He went on about his business and then returned to fulfill his promise. Fortunately for him, the woman was in the very spot-waiting, as it were, for his return- however, something terrible had taken place. Every word he spoke to that woman seemed to be of no avail. His words bounced right on her ear- lobe and fell to the floor, it seemed. The Spirit quietly taught my friend that he had missed the moment when her heart was softened for the Word. The moment he chose was not the moment of God. Of course, this experience had him feeling guilty for quite a while.

Like this pastor, many of us have missed our moments with the Lord. The correct time eluded us because we procrastinated. One wise person said that procrastination is the thief of time a thief as the Devil himself is. "The thief cometh not, but for to steal, and to kill and to destroy…" (St. John 10:10) KJV. This is his secret wile, which he uses to steal blessings.

Before we got saved, many of us put off this compulsory decision of the soul for minutes, hours, days, weeks, or even years. We knew that we had to get saved but oh, the many excuses that surfaced. The Devil knew we had limited time, but he still beckoned us to put it off. We knew this was the way to the better life, but the Devil said, "Wait."

Many times, we miss our season, and as it is in the natural, one season takes a particular period of time to return. Many of us have had delayed birthing in our spiritual gifts because of procrastination.

The God we serve is a God who works often with movement punctuated by the word *quickly*. This is a tendency that is consistent with the movement of God. Of course, he is the same God that bids us to wait for instruction, but as soon as this is given, we must move *quickly*. In the King James Version, this word is often used in conjunction with a command or instruction God had given.

In my own mind, the word *quickly* means 'to move or take action promptly, immediately, speedily.' The meaning of the word *procrastinate* is 'put off; postpone' or 'to drag your feet.' This clearly teaches that these two words or attitudes cannot exist together in the same instance. They are as opposite as faith and fear.

> Procrastination is the thief of time, and the Devil is
> a *thief.*

Let us take a look at the usage of the word *quickly* in Scriptures.

1. God pondered over the matter of keeping as a secret the
    impending destruction of Sodom and Gomorrah. He thought
    to himself whether or not to keep this secret from his friend-
    Abraham. However, He finally came to the decision that he
    wouldn't because of what Psalm 25:14 says, "The secret of the
    LORD is with them that fear him." God then went down to
    the abode of Abraham with some angels, intending to speak
    with this, his friend. Upon seeing the heavenly strangers,
    Abraham, desiring to maintain the presence of these visitors,
    gave his wife an instruction that was of utmost importance.

"And Abraham hastened into the tent unto Sarah, and said, make
ready quickly three measures of fine meal, knead it, and make cakes upon
the hearth" (Genesis 18:6).

Now consider what could have happened had Sarah tarried, dragged
her feet, or waited before she took heed to the instructions of Abraham.
The word that would build up the faith in her to cause the conception
of Isaac would not have been delivered (Genesis 18:14). She was in the
kitchen, preparing the sacrifice, when this word was spoken. She was in
a close enough range to hear the word—the right place at the right time.
Bearing in mind that a sacrifice sustains the presence of God (God lives in
the praises of his people, which is a sacrifice), Abraham would have missed
his appointment with God. Procrastination would have robbed Abraham
and Sarah of the blessings.

2. In Numbers 16:46, as the children of Israel murmured against
    Moses and Aaron for the killing of some ungodly men, a
    plague from the Lord fell upon them. Moses then instructed
    Aaron using this very prompting word.

"Take a censer, and put fire therein from off the altar, and put on
incense, and go quickly unto the congregation, and make an atonement

for them: for there is wrath gone out from the LORD; the plague is begun" (Numbers 16:46).

In this second instance, as the plague came out from the Lord against Israel, Moses realized the urgency which was required to save the people's lives, since God had clearly told him to move from among the people so that God could destroy them. What if Aaron had procrastinated like some of us? Many more that 14,700 people would have died. Yes, that is how many died, even though Aaron did move quickly.

3.   While David ran from Absalom, who wanted to kill him, the Lord allowed Hushai to be privy to the capture plan, and it was told to Abiathar.

"Now therefore send quickly, and tell David, saying, 'Lodge not this night in the plains of the wilderness, but speedily pass over; lest the king be swallowed up, and all the people that are with him'" (II Samuel 17:16).

How many would have died had David not heeded the command he received? David took action quickly and passed over Jordon. The scriptures said in II Samuel 17:22, "there lacked not one of them that was not gone over Jordon." Not one was harmed. The enemy that counselled Absalom, Ahithophel, died instead of David and his people. He hanged himself (II Samuel 17:23).

4.   As Jonathan sought to get David out of the hands of his father, he gave him instruction about how to escape. He told him, "And when thou hast stayed three days, then thou shalt go down quickly, and come to the place where thou didst hide thyself when the business was in hand, and shalt remain by the stone Ezel" (I Samuel 20:19).

Jonathan's plan with David was a good one, but without proper execution it would have failed. David hurried and got in and out of Nob in time to escape the wrath of Saul, who commanded the killing of an entire set of priests because David eluded him. Now, imagine the outcome if the action of speed didn't modify David's movements.

5. As Jesus spake a parable to his disciples about the coming of the kingdom of God, there was a command given that desired urgency.

"Go out quickly into the streets and lanes of the city, and bring in hither the poor, and the maimed, and the halt, and the blind" (St. Luke 14:21).

There are illustrations of the usage of the word *quickly* in many other Scriptures, such as Genesis 27:20, Exodus 32:8, Deuteronomy 9:3; 9:12; 9:16; 11:17; 28:20, Joshua 2:5; 8:19; 10:6; 23:16, Jude 2:17, II Kings 1:11, II Chronicles 18:8, Ecclesiastes 4:12 and other New Testament Scriptures.

The instruction of God must not be delayed in its action state. It must be carried out as quickly as it is given unless instructed otherwise. The Spirit realm is constantly bombarded with the travel of demonic forces. If we do not move in the appointed time, the way that once was opened can become closed and be a lost opportunity.

Knowing that to procrastinate with the things of God is actually not of God, you may want to find out why you are so apt to fall to it or how to avoid procrastinating.

Part II

THE ROOT CAUSES OF PROCRASTINATION

What causes so many of us saved folks to fall to this wile of Procrastination? I would say the main cause is the evil heart of- Doubt. Doubt as to whether or not God spoke. In order to overcome the wile of procrastination, we must learn how to counteract its root causes. We know that if we kill the root then we basically kill the tree. But before we can kill the root it must first be identified. We will therefore first look at doubt as one of the root causes of procrastination.

Common complaint

So many times I have heard persons complain about the inability to distinguish between the voice of God and their own mind's thoughts. But this is an unnecessary dilemna. Firstly, so many of us are quick to say that a bad thought came from the enemy. As soon as it passes through our minds we say, 'here comes the Devil.' On the contrary, when a good thought comes, we are quick to say it is from our minds. Were not our minds at enmity with God? So aren't we more likely to think evil thoughts than good? Why then do we ascribe all bad thoughts to Satan but are reluctant to give credit to God for the good ones?

> It is more reasonable to ascribe good thoughts to God than to ourselves.

Fear God

On the other hand, some persons procrastinate because they lack the fear of the Lord. The scriptures say that the fear of the Lord is the beginning of wisdom. Therefore if we fear God then we would be wise enough to respond promptly to His instructions or as soon as we are certain that it comes from him.

Another cause for procrastination is the human tendency to be lazy. How often has the Lord called us to rise up early and pray but we choose rather to spend 10 minutes more sleeping? But what comparison is 10 minutes sleep to the eternal benefits of a minute prayer?

> What comparison is 10 minutes sleep to the eternal value of a minute prayer?

We therefore need a change of attitude towards the things of God and to God himself. His sheep know his voice and we show that we love him when we do what he commands.

Part III

How to KILL THE ROOTS OF Procrastination

The parable spoken by Jesus concerning the marriage supper is very dynamic. The command concerning responding quickly has to do with the fact that the Lord cometh quickly. "Behold, I come quickly: hold that fast which thou hast, that no man take thy crown" (Revelations 3:11). It is for the church to know that in this time and age there has to be more urgency in the gathering of the harvest because the day of the Lord is at hand. "The night is far spent, the day is at hand: let us therefore cast off the works of darkness, and let us put on the armour of light" (Romans 13:12). If this gathering is not done quickly then many will be left out.

This parable speaks to gathering others (Gentiles) because the children (Israelites) were not ready.

Haste has to be made because the Gentiles are many but labourers are few. "… The harvest truly is plenteous, but the labourers are few" (St. Matthew 9:37). In this incident, there was no doubt in the disciples mind about what the Lord was saying or even more importantly- who was speaking because the Lord was standing right in front of them. We however have to listen for his voice in the Spirit and this poses the challenge for many. Even though his voice is like none other and is clearly distinguishable for the mature sheep, others of us still struggle to make the distinction. We will therefore discuss this matter of the voice of God. My hope is that in identifying the voice of God we will be motivated to move quickly at his command.

If procrastination in you is caused by doubt then it is easy to overcome same. To kill doubt as to whether or not you are hearing from God you must be aware of the following principles:

The voice of God

Firstly, because God confirms whatever word he sends to you then he is easy to discern. If you are having a challenge determining whether or not God has instructed you to do something just simply ask Him to confirm His word. Our loving father has no problem measuring up to His own written word since it says "In the mouth of two or three witnesses shall every word be established" (II Corinthians 13:1). He has even asked us to "...try him and prove him..." (Malachi 3:10). I have had many

> God always confirms his words.

experiences which taught me how to discern the voice of God. I will share them with you for perhaps you have had similar experiences and have not even realized that it was the voice of God.

God's voice in prayer

At the beginning of this assignment as I prayed about the writing of this book, I was asking God about what the book should be entitled. Well, amidst my prayer came the words on our tongue, "The wiles of the Devil". I spoke them before they got into my mind and so I knew it was from the Spirit.

His voice through prophecy

When God gave me the desire to write this book, I was comfortable with the thought. I was also very eager to begin the process. I had by that time become somewhat matured in identifying the desires of God for my life and so as soon as I got the name of the book, I started writing. However, I got lackadaisical along the way and so I did not write for about a month and a half. One Sunday afternoon a Canadian preacher spoke at my church in Jamaica and as he was through preaching, he asked that all the saints gather at the altar. He prayed for the brothers and encouraged them. He then fixed his eyes on me and told the church to listen. He said, "This girl (referring to me) has got a book to write." Then he looked at me and said: "The Lord said that the word is in you. Write the book." That confirmation encouraged my heart so much that I was pushed into writing line after line. The word of prophecy confirmed the voice of God.

As I said earlier, God speaks to us directly at times. He has a way of doing the same thing a million different ways and so you may find that he speaks to you differently in similar situations.

His voice in wisdom

When God first spoke to me in this particular way, it was different from all the other times. It was forceful yet simple. It came in the form of a deep understanding that occurred suddenly; it was one morning within a year of being saved while I was in Teacher's College. Back then, I was a boarder. The persons in boarding would rise from bed and gather at the school's cafeteria for breakfast. I remember distinctly, that as I got up out of my bed and was about to move away from the bed that a deep and sudden understanding hit my consciousness that "Without God, I can do nothing". Along with this understanding came what seemed to have been a packet of explanation and so I got the whole revelation that -if God does not enable me Spiritually then there is nothing that I can do. Because I was an avid reader of Christian Literature, I could remember having read that if God speaks to you then his written word will confirm it and so my memory testified that this understanding matched up with scriptures:

"I can do all things **through Christ which strengtheneth me**" (Philippians 4:13) and "I thank Christ Jesus our Lord, **who hath enabled me**, for that he counted me faithful, putting me into the ministry…" (I Timothy 1:12). Many other scriptures confirmed that this was from God. There is yet another way that he speaks.

God's voice in a thought

My next experiencing of God's voice was more forceful. I remember one morning as I was on our way to class that the reality of the Hymen, which establishes virginity in a female, came to my mind. I questioned the Lord about the importance of this thin layer of blood. Studies have shown that there are no biological functions of this membrane. My line of questioning was based on the fact that I could not see the importance of this 'thing' which once it is broken can never be repaired and is just there only to be ruptured.

So I asked God about the necessity of the hymen. The response was a smooth but forceful thought that came from somewhere else. The thought was, 'it is there to symbolize the sealing of the covenant between a man and his wife.' Which meant that upon having sexual intercourse and shedding the blood of the hymen, the husband and wife would have sealed their covenant? Immediately it came back to my mind that a covenant (as marriage is) is sealed with the shedding of blood. This is confirmed in the following scriptures:

> "For a testament is of force after men are dead: otherwise it is of no strength at all while the testator liveth. Whereupon neither the first testament was dedicated **without blood.** For when Moses had spoken every precept to all the people according to the law, he took the blood of calves and of goats, with water, and scarlet wool, and hyssop, and sprinkled both the book, and all the people, saying, **this is the blood of the testament** which God hath enjoined unto you" (Hebrews 9:17).

This is not to say that the wedding covenant is not sealed if the woman has no hymen for it is well known in the medical arena that some woman are born without a hymen and that some women's hymen stay intact even after they have had sexual relations.

Other females' hymens get broken from strenuous exercises. The understanding here is that the natural things are showing the things of the Spirit and so if this hymen was only present in a single woman, the purpose for it would still hold true just as a man who is born blind is still a human being even though he lacks one characteristic of the ideal."

Let's move on.

God laughed

Another time when God communicated directly with me, it was very unusual. I was in my room back in College one day and feeling so available to God that I said to Him. "God, humble me". A laugh came up in my Spirit and I knew that God had laughed. I did not quite understand this but it made me laugh too. I called a friend of mine and shared this experience with him. He responded by laughing when I told him what I had said to God. He said that I would not want God to humble me because the scripture says that he humbled Israel then fed them. My friend said it would be more appropriate to ask God to help me to be humble. God has a sense of humor.

> God has a sense of humor.

These instances prove to me that God deals with us according to our faith. God, knowing that our faith is weak will not deal with us as he would with a person whose faith is strong. I knew for example that if God had spoken to me in the initial stages of my walk with Him in the way that he gave me the name of the book then I probably would not have recognized it as the voice of God.

Even though God uses different methods to speak to us, it is all unified in that; it always matches with the scriptures. Also, when you make listening to Him habitual, you know His voice.

"My sheep hear my voice, and I know them, and they follow me" (St. John 10:27).

Distinguishing the voice of God

If you cannot associate with any of the experiences shared and you are still having challenges distinguishing the voice of God then there is yet another method to kill doubt. Ask someone who is more mature than you are about the things of God. There are many elders around you. They may not attend your local church but once that person is Spiritual and you see their fruits, go ahead and get their help. God knows that we will have times when we will need to be fed into maturity and so that is why the strong are encouraged to strengthen the weak. Share your experiences with the elder you have chosen and let that one guide you.

There is an example in scripture which suits this method I have prescribed. This is a well known bible story in which the more mature helped the younger. This is seen in the story of Eli and Samuel. We know about Hanna's inability to have children and the ridicule she went through because of this. However, after she sought God earnestly, she was blessed with a son whom she had vowed to give back to the Lord. As soon as Samuel was weaned from the breast, he was therefore brought to the temple where he was left in the care of Eli, the priest. Though this young lad grew up in the house of God and watched the elders carry out the duties of the temple; he was not familiar with the voice of God. Therefore when Samuel first heard the voice of the Lord as a boy he did not know that it was God. He simply communicated his experience to Eli who was able to offer spiritual direction and so Samuel responded to God's calling.

"And it came to pass at that time, when Eli was laid down in his place, and his eyes began to wax dim, that he could not see; And ere the lamp of God went out in the temple of the Lord, where the ark of God was, and Samuel was laid down to sleep; That the Lord called Samuel: and he answered, here am I. And he ran unto Eli, and said, Here am I; for thou calledst me. And he said I called not; lie down again. And he went and lay down. And the Lord called yet again, Samuel. And Samuel arose and went to Eli, and said, here am I; for thou didst call me. And he answered, I called not, our son; lie down again. Now Samuel did not yet know the Lord, neither was the Word of the Lord yet revealed unto him. And the Lord called Samuel again the third time. And he arose and went to Eli, and said, here am I; for thou didst call me. And Eli perceived that the Lord had called the child. Therefore Eli said unto Samuel, Go, lie down: and it shall be, if he call thee, that thou shalt say, Speak, Lord; for thy servant heareth. So Samuel went and lay down in his place. And the Lord came, and stood, and called as at other times, Samuel, Samuel. Then Samuel answered, Speak; for thy servant heareth. And the Lord said to Samuel, Behold, I will do a thing in Israel, at which both the ears of every one that heareth it shall tingle" (I Samuel 3:2-11).

It is a principle that holds true today. Get help from the matured and get rid of doubt. Kill it!

Killing doubt

If your procrastinating is not caused by doubt then it may very well be caused by a lack of 'the fear of the Lord'. If you truly understand the magnitude and the power of God then you will not hesitate at His instructions. Just the thought that He can get us out of the way should be enough to get us moving. Consider these scriptures:

"For the pillars of the earth are the LORD'S, and he hath set the world upon them" (I Samuels2:8).

"It is he that sitteth upon the circle of the earth, and the inhabitants thereof are as grasshoppers; that stretcheth out the heavens as a curtain, and spreadeth them out as a tent to dwell in" (Isaiah 40:22).

"But will God in very deed dwell with men on the earth? Behold, heaven and the heaven of heavens cannot contain thee; how much less this house which I have built!" (II Chronicles 6:18).

"And the channels of the sea appeared, the foundations of the world were discovered, at the rebuking of the LORD, at the blast of the breath of his nostrils" (II Samuels 22:16).

On the more tender side, if you truly understand that there is someone out there who is living a better Christian life than you are living, serving God longer than you have been serving Him and is more willing to obey His commands, then you should feel extra special to hear his voice. You need to see that it is His purpose for and calling on your life that keeps Him calling on you to operate. If you understand this then you will move immediately at his command. Of all the things that God has taken the time to do for you, you should be willing to do the reasonable thing which is to follow his instructions. To kill this root just listen to this song writer who penned these words:

"He took the time to die on the cross

So that your soul would not be lost

If you find yourself slipping in the things you do

Take time out for Jesus, he took the time for you."

Christ gave up his life that we might live; therefore he desires to live his life through us. "And that he died for all, that they which live should not henceforth live unto themselves, but unto him which died for them, and rose again" (II Corinthians 5:15). We are his hands and feet and therefore we should be willing to avail ourselves for His using. After all, we are not our own. We belong to Jesus.

"Forasmuch as ye know that ye were not redeemed with corruptible things, as silver and gold, from your vain conversation received by tradition from your fathers; but with the precious blood of Christ, as of a lamb without blemish and without spot" (II Pter1:18-19).

It is the same appeal that Apostle Paul makes to us to be reasonable when he speaks in Romans 12. We, as stewards of the time which God has afforded us, must use it wisely and in the way that God directs.

The Devil uses this wile effectively by crowding our minds with doubt and carelessness. However, we can shake off his cunning and subtle tricks with the Word of God. After all, "How shall a young man cleanse his way? By taking heed thereto according to thy word" (Psalm 119:9).

Chapter Two

The wile of "Impatience"

One should wait patiently upon the Lord then only after he gives instructions should one move quickly.

The kingdom of God is governed by rules and regulations which makes it difficult for many persons to cope. This is so because many of us are accustomed to calling all the shots in our lives as well as in the lives of those around us. We like to make things happen in our timing and stop things when we are satisfied with their end and so we abhor anything else. However, the church is built by God and so he lays things in place according to his pre- ordained timing. If therefore we are a part of the holy habitation of God we must be willing to allow him to move in our lives in His time. The principle of time is of great significance to the Kingdom of God.

> The principle of time is one of great significance to the Kingdom of God.

The Lord who is eternal, created a slot in eternity called time. This slot has both a beginning and an end. God regulates everything in time on his own clock. With God, nothing happens before the time. This can be seen in the creation story where God made the grass then the animals and he was careful to make the sea creatures before he made the birds because some birds feed on fishes. So God does everything in perfect timing.

The wile of impatience implies that our thoughts are higher than the thoughts of God and that God is not a good time keeper. We get impatient because somehow it seems that God takes too long. The secret to success is waiting upon the timing of the almighty God. "But they that wait on the Lord shall renew their strength; they shall mount up with wings as eagles; they shall run, and not be weary; and they shall walk, and not faint" (Isaiah 40:31).

> The secret to success is waiting upon the timing of the almighty God

In the scriptures we see the danger of impatience. In the situation with Abraham as he journeyed to his land to which the Lord had called him, he was instructed not to go down to Egypt. However, as he journeyed, there was a famine in the land and instead of waiting on the provision of God, he decided to journey off into Egypt. This led to a sharp rebuke and he lost much grounds. When Abraham should have been moving along he had to be journeying back to the spot from where he had detoured.

Impatience also caused King Saul his kingdom for as he waited for a message from God through Samuel he became impatient and decided to carry out a priestly duty though he was not a priest. Saul thought that if he made the sacrifice then he would get an answer more promptly than in the timing that God had predetermined. However this was not pleasing to God, so God sent him an unfavorable message.

"And Samuel said to Saul, You have done foolishly: you have not kept the commandment of the Lord your God, which he commanded you: for now would the Lord have established your kingdom on Israel for ever. But now your kingdom shall not continue: the Lord has sought him a man after his own heart, and the Lord has commanded him to be captain over his people, because you have not kept that which the Lord commanded you" (I Samuel 13:13).

Picture of Patience

Though the Israelites are most often bashed for their murmuring and complaining, there was a lovely picture of patience painted by the Holy

Spirit. As the Israelites journeyed through the wilderness being led by God, they waited for him to show them where to go and exactly when to move.

"And on the day that the tabernacle was reared up the cloud covered the tabernacle, namely, the tent of the testimony: and at even there was on the tabernacle as it were the appearance of fire, until the morning. So it was always: the cloud covered it by day, and the appearance of fire by night. And when the cloud was taken up from the tabernacle, then after that the children of Israel journeyed: and in the place where the cloud stayed, there the children of Israel pitched their tents. At the commandment of the Lord the children of Israel journeyed, and at the commandment of the Lord they pitched: as long as the cloud stayed on the tabernacle they rested in their tents. And when the cloud tarried long on the tabernacle many days, then the children of Israel kept the charge of the Lord, and journeyed not. And so it was, when the cloud was a few days on the tabernacle; according to the commandment of the Lord they stayed in their tents, and according to the commandment of the Lord they journeyed. And so it was, when the cloud stayed from even to the morning, and that the cloud was taken up in the morning, then they journeyed: whether it was by day or by night that the cloud was taken up, they journeyed. Or whether it were two days, or a month, or a year, that the cloud tarried on the tabernacle, remaining thereon, the children of Israel stayed in their tents, and journeyed not: but when it was taken up, they journeyed. At the commandment of the Lord they rested in the tents, and at the commandment of the Lord they journeyed: they kept the charge of the Lord, at the commandment of the Lord by the hand of Moses" (Numbers 9:15).

One can imagine how tedious it must have been for so many people to keep their composure out in the wilderness where they were vulnerable to so much. They also knew the way to the land of promise for, had they not known it then the 12 spies could not have found Canaan and returned to them with a report. This further shows that they had the opportunity to run ahead of God but they did not.

If the Israelites had tried to out run God then all lives could have been lost. They had physical evidence of the enemies around but we cannot see our enemies with our naked eyes; all the greater reason for us to depend on him, who is Spirit and discerns all this. He will lead us into the safe way when the time is right.

One thing that impatience does is that it puts us in a place before the time. In this place we are unprepared because the tools for that situation are not yet given. Impatience has a way of delivering to us things that we cannot handle and they have to be incubated until the time of the promise. Due to this incubation and not natural development, the promise does not shine as it was meant to. It is like one born out of season.

> Impatience has a way of delivering to us things that we are not prepared for

Impatience also puts us in a place that was not prepared for us for as Moses said "… Rise up, LORD, and let your enemies be scattered; and let them that hate you flee before you. And when it rested, he said, Return, O LORD, to the many thousands of Israel" (Numbers 10:35-36).

God goes before us and when the way is clear, he then returns to lead us into the way that we ought to go. Therefore if we move before God moves then we are in danger because we would be outside of the protection of God.

Part II

Why are we so vulnerable to impatience?

In a hurry

The enemy knows that humans always seem to be in haste. We hurry because we tend to believe that time is not on our side. The world system teaches us that time is money. Hence, members of the human population who the world calls 'successful prospects' are always in a haste to reach their goals. God is so different because the scripture declares that:

"But, beloved, be not ignorant of this one thing, that one day is with the Lord as a thousand years, and a thousand years as one day" (II Peter 3:8).

Anecdote

I can remember when God led me into starting my personal business and I had to source a particular piece of raw material that was instrumental to my operations. I shopped around but as I waited on the Lord in patience, I soon found other suppliers who delivered the product for three times less. Such a wait created the prospect for my business to take off with a bang and to become a major profitable entity within a short time.

The rewiring

We need a total rewiring to work on the system of God. He is in no haste to deliver his promises because he knows our end and whatever he has planned for us is achievable in the time span of our lives. Hence if God has it planned for us to be married with children then the length of our days are perfect to match the achievement of these plans. Therefore, after this assurance is given by God, which he often gives, then it is just time to continue our present assigned task and wait.

> If God has it planned for us then it is ours

We humans often measure ourselves against the works of others and so we tend to try to achieve more than we were made to because we covet another person's work. This often leads us off into areas that were not divinely slated for us and so we end up with a strain. It is very much like a rat trying to carry the burden of a donkey. In so doing, we tend to expect God to rubber stamp our decisions after they have been made instead of acknowledging him and allowing him to direct our path. We assume impatiently that because he has not yet answered, his silence means consent; another mistake that can cost us life.

Pressures of life

Another reason we fall into this wile of impatience is because the Devil places us under extreme pressure until we feel as if we are going to crack if we do not act. However it is in these situations that it is time to stand still and see the salvation of the Lord. There is a story discussed in later chapters in which David ran from Saul, he was totally surrounded by Saul and his men. In a moment when all seemed to be over, David waited, then lo and behold there came news that the Philistines had invaded Israel. Saul and his men had to return home. Can you imagine what could have happened if David had not waited on the Lord? He probably would have moved foolishly. In that moment all he did and was supposed to do was to wait upon the Lord. Just in waiting, Saul had to retreat from chasing the man of God.

> When God has said nothing, wait, he is about to do something

Has God forgotten?

We also have the tendency to believe that God has forgotten us and our stage in life. If we truly reflect on who God is then we will know that this is never so. We tend to forget that we serve a God who says our walls are ever before him or that he has engraved us on the palm of his hand or that he counts the stars and calls them by name or even that he numbers the hair on our heads and most intricately that he takes note of every soulless sparrow that dies. If we truly keep these things in mind then we will always be assured that he has his eye on us. This means that he remembers us.

We get impatient because we do not trust the omniscience of God. Neither do we fully trust his love for us; for if we trust him then we will know that he does not leave us nor forsake us. We will know that He who takes thought for a single sparrow will take thought for us.

God knows and remembers all things well

Part III

DESTROYING THE ROOTS OF impatience

The root cause of impatience is a lack of trust in the almighty God. We serve a God who swears that heaven and earth shall pass away before one drop of his Word shall pass. *Matthew 24:35, Mark 13:31, Luke 21:33.* He promises that if we delight ourselves in him then he will give us the desire of our hearts according to *Psalm 37:4.* God is a God who respects time. All the plans he has for us are on a time clock. "For I know the thoughts that I think toward you, said the Lord, thoughts of peace, and not of evil, to give you an expected end" (Jeremiah 29:11). If we therefore develop a confidence in God that whatever he says, he will bring it to pass then we will do well. One way of the Lord is- the habit of declaring something, daring the Devil to stop it, then bringing it to pass. Whatever the Lord has promised us it is ours and the Devil can only delay it as he did the answer to Daniel's prayer. However, as soon as an angel goes warring the victory will be ours and God's timing will still be perfect.

The 23rd Psalm has worked wonders in the lives of many but the note that strikes the sweetest strain in my heart is the final word when it is sung- AMEN. All that was said in that Psalm, before the Devil could add anything to it, the Spirit says amen. Jesus is truly the author and finisher of our faith and so the Devil can only make suggestions and creative misperceptions but our fate is determined by Christ.

The Spirit and me

At the genesis of my ministry, the Lord allowed me to preach exceptionally well judging by the spiritual response of the congregants and the spiritual empowerment that engulfed me. Many times after that I have sought to do the same but it has not yet materialized. The Spirit has ministered to me that he was giving me a glimpse into his future plans for me. God has promised me that there is greatness in me. He has given me long term and short time promises. He ministered to me that, 'in bringing the short term promises to pass then it builds my faith and patience to wait on the long term promises.' Many times when I got low in the Spirit, God just reminded me of the plans that he has for me. This usually brings an excitement in my Spirit which rekindles my fire. I know I shall not die until God has delivered his promises. This is so seared into my Spirit that even in my dreams when I am sentenced to death, I have confidence that God will make a way and he always does. This is the hope of every believer. "The promises of God are yea and yea and amen" (II Corinthians 1:20).

> The promises of God are yea and yea and AMEN

Whenever God makes a promise, it is for us to pray for its fulfillment then live on until he brings it to pass. For as sure as the night follows the day, the Word of God will not return unto him void. There are some things that the Lord has said that are a must. "Being confident of this very thing that he which has begun a good work in you will perform it until the day of Jesus Christ..." (Philippians 1:6)

We need to trust the Lord that whatever plans he has for us and wherever He has placed us at the present time is where we will best thrive. This means that where we are physically is the place where we can best bear fruits and there is nowhere else on earth more fertile for us in this moment. If we then appreciate the things we have in that way then surely we can be content. I remember back in College when I started to become settled in the Lord, when the bus would leave me by a minute or a plan failed, I would just say it is the work of the Lord and I am on His timing; for in taking things that way, I developed contentment and a deep relationship with Him. It is not enough to know that God is with us. It is even greater to acknowledge his presence in our every move.

Let us wait upon the Lord, be of good courage so that he shall strengthen our hearts.

Points to build on:
1.   Once God has spoken, move quickly
2.   Until God has spoken, wait patiently

Chapter Three

The wile of Addiction

For most of us we have at some time in our lives been addicted to one thing or another. For me it has been Pepsi, Malta, Cranberry juices, Banana chips, all at different times of course. Food can become a problem if we as children of God get addicted. These foods can destroy the temple as well as prevent us from enjoying our feast of prayer or even worse, fasting times. Good for me it was mostly food items to which I have been addicted and so losing these addictions was quite simple. All I had to do was to overdose on that item then I would get cloyed and like it no more. Becoming cloyed meant the end of a food addiction; at least for that season. For other addictions it is not so easy.

People have in many cultures and across many countries been enslaved by their addictions. Some have been addicted to drugs, sex, people, work; unhealthy habits just to mention a few; All of these addictions have led to destruction of some kind; death, sex crimes, family conflict, emotional trauma and lifestyle diseases.

In the Kingdom of God, additions are also prevalent. This is so because this gives the Devil a great level of control in our lives.

Defined

Addiction sets a path for itself. This means that once a person has reached the stage of addiction then there is no more a need for external motivation since the object of the addiction has a grasp on the addict's consciousness. The Devil therefore works to get the children of God to be addicted to soul destructive practices so that a never ending cycle can begin. Addictions start as small habits and soon grow into oversized slave masters.

Good addiction

Addictions can be towards the things of the Kingdom but it can also be towards things of the world. The latter is when it becomes dangerous. Whatever the addiction, the person becomes the slave of the Spirit behind it. Therefore, if we are addicted to the things of God then we become the servants of God. However, if we become addicted to the things of the world then we become servants of the god of this world, who is Satan according to II Corinthian 4:4. One case of addiction to the things of God is seen in I Corinthians 16:15 where Paul highlighted the addiction of some saints by saying: "I beseech you, brethren, (you know the house of Stephanas, that it is the first fruits of Achaia, and that they have addicted themselves to the ministry of the saints)." These saints were drawn and enslaved to a good thing. Good things cause the soul to flourish but the bad things drain the soul of life.

We must overcome Addictions

An addiction does not disappear; it has to be conquered. For instance, some young people get addicted to sex and hence they fornicate. Some run into marriage instead of surrendering to God and getting rid of this Spirit. When they marry, something remarkable happens. The Spirit of fornication turns the addict over to a Spirit of adultery and the process goes on. One needs to stop and deal with his or her addictions by asking the Lord for strength to overcome same and working earnestly at overcoming this destructive element.

Anecdote

The story is told of a young Evangelist who was very gifted and anointed. The leaders of her church became concerned when she was hasty in her desire to marry a new convert. The story goes that they had been going together for a while and had been involved in a sexual relationship.

She tried to get it sealed by getting him into the church so that they could get married. The leaders tried to persuade her to wait a while so that they could observe whether or not the new convert was serious about serving the lord. However, being pressed by her addiction to fornicate, she swore that she would leave her post as Evangelist if she were not allowed to marry this object of her addiction. The wedding went through but a few months later she met in an accident on her way out with another man in a bid to feed her adulterous addiction. She stepped out of church and this accident left her with a permanent deformity.

Illustrated

There are also some characters in the bible who displayed addictions, some even unto death. Noah displayed an addiction. We see where this bible stalwart got so drunk that he became a stumbling block for his son Ham. This is recorded in Genesis 9:20-25.

"And Noah began to be a farmer, and he planted a vineyard: And he drank of the wine, and was drunken; and he was uncovered within his tent. And Ham, the father of Canaan, saw the nakedness of his father, and told his two brothers without. And Shem and Japheth took a garment, and laid it on both their shoulders, and went backward, and covered the nakedness of their father; and their faces were backward, and they saw not their father's nakedness. And Noah awoke from his wine, and knew what his younger son had done to him. And he said, Cursed be Canaan; a servant of servants shall he be to his brothers."

If Noah had not fallen then Ham would not have been cursed. Theologians even believe that this curse on Ham influenced his descendant Nimrod who was master mind behind the tower of Babel. This goes to show how addiction affects the children of the addict. Spirits move from generation to generation and the consequences of the parent's actions bring trouble for the following generation. Many times when we meet drunkards and gamblers, they report that their parents had the same vices.

The great King Solomon also got hooked by this wile. From the beginning, it was ordained that a man would have one wife. As time progressed, we see where Abraham and other patriarchs took wives to themselves. God did not interrupt such practices but of course they were not in his perfect will. Whenever man breaks the hedge that God sets about them then the serpent will bite according to Ecclesiastes 10:8. The great and wise king Solomon became foolish by addiction. The earliest report of Solomon taking a pagan wife was when he married the daughter of a Pharaoh. He then became so enslaved by his sexual greed that he later took hundreds of other wives plus concubines. This addiction got so intense that the Bible reports the following:

> "And he had seven hundred wives, princesses, and three hundred concubines: and his wives turned away his heart. For it came to pass, when Solomon was old, that his wives turned away his heart after other gods: and his heart was not perfect with the Lord his God, as was the heart of David his father. For Solomon went after Ashtoreth the goddess of the Zidonians, and after Milcom the abomination of the Ammonites. And Solomon did evil in the sight of the Lord, and went not fully after the Lord, as did David his father. Then did Solomon build an high place for Chemosh, the abomination of Moab, in the hill that is before Jerusalem, and for Molech, the abomination of the children of Ammon. And likewise did he for all his strange wives, which burnt incense and sacrificed unto their gods. And the Lord was angry with Solomon, because his heart was turned from the Lord God of Israel, which had appeared unto him twice" (I Kings 11: 3).

The addiction of Solomon soon had him turning away from the ways of God. Once addiction sets in the heart, it takes over the mind and then rules the members of the body. Solomon got so addicted that his rational was absent though he was the wisest man ever. This leads me to say that if the wisest man was not exempt from such an addiction and could even be tricked and enslaved to it, then why do we think that we are immune? The Devil attacks the Bible's great characters to show his strength. This is so because it is well known that a fighter is stronger than the strongest opponent he overcomes. However, as a born again child of God, there is no need to fear because it is said that "…greater is he that is in you, than he that is in the world" (I John 4:4).

To every negative addiction is attached a demon. The role of this demon is to maintain the strong hold. A strong hold refers to 'keeping guard of territory and preventing anything that will weaken the defenses.' The demon reminds the addicted that he or she needs the object of the addiction and persuades the addict that losing the object will mean the end of life or will erase the reason for living.

I am almost certain that you can relate to this. Some persons may say that I am mistaken for making the previous statement but I am not. The only thing or person that one should ever feel it impossible to live without is God almighty. Anything else that draws this feeling is an idol which may have been created through addiction.

Part II

Why are we so prone to Addiction?

We are prone to addictions because they are bred out of regular life style practices. Addictions are connected to the flesh which "lusteth against our Spirit" according to Galatians 5:17 and which "lusteth to envy" (James 4:5). Also the flesh connects us to the world around us. The flesh creates connections through associations. We know people by the way they speak, feel, smell, look etc. The bond begins to form when the flesh is tickled by the object which brings it satisfaction. Having lived in this flesh for many years, it becomes very easy to react to its impulses for, before we knew God, this was our sole prerogative- to satisfy flesh.

Whatever pleases the flesh and is done routinely soon becomes a habit. A habit is that which is done almost thoughtlessly and becomes routine. One popular adage is "habits are easy to make and hard to break; for if you take off the H you still have ABIT, if you take off the HA you still have BIT, if you take off the HAB you still have IT." Addiction is one step up from a habit. This is said because while a habit can be lost through change of practice or environment, addictions follow us around and dictates to us whatever it pleases.

We are prone to becoming addicts because the flesh is a slave master. There are many appetites in us humans but the one which the Devil attacks the most is the sexual appetite for it is the most natural common denominator in humans- both great and small.

Illustration

The idea of the opening of the appetite is best demonstrated in a full course meal. That which is served first is used to stimulate the appetite so that the rest of the meal becomes enjoyable. In this very way the Devil serves up appetizers in our movies, workplace and other surroundings to stimulate the fleshly appetites. Once the appetite has been stimulated, he introduces the real meal. Christians whet their appetites all the time with the Devil's treats and then expect to be able to resist the meal.

Many of us came into the kingdom with addictions but soon weaned them as we improved in Spiritual awareness and practices. Others of us nurtured these addictions until they became so unbearable that they almost strangled us. It is said that skeletons in the closet soon stink and disgrace us. We humans tend to believe that we can keep things hidden forever but had this been possible, the Devil would not have introduced it in the first place. The Devil's aim is to steal, kill and destroy. We fail to understand this and so we take his bait and fall prey to his treats which lead only to death. We should also remember that that which is done in secret SHALL be proclaimed on the house top according to Matthew 4:22.

Discussion

One of my students once asked if she could take a particular object of her affections over into the kingdom once she got saved. The Spirit gave me a simple answer for her. 'That which is chosen when the eyes are blinded may very well be distasteful when the eyes are opened.' This is truly the reality because whatever the Devil provides as we grope in the darkness of sin was meant to destroy us and so sooner or later, more so later, it will show its true colours and cause us torment and sorrows. If we believe this then we will stay clear of youthful lust.

Part III

Eradicating addiction

There is one main piece of amour to use in the fight against addictions. This is the breastplate of righteousness. Righteousness refers to right principles and standards and since there is only one way to righteousness, we have to internalize the WORD of God. If we do not know God's word then we cannot withstand this fiery dart. Righteousness is called a breastplate because once the breast is covered there is protection for vital organs. In that very sense, the Spiritual breastplate of righteousness protects vital Spiritual organs especially the heart which is synonymous to the mind with which we serve the Lord as stated in Romans 7:25. We first need to cleanse our minds by renewing it. The bible bids us to be renewed in the Spirit of our minds as taught in Ephesians 4:23. This means changing the Spirit with which the mind thinks. The mind of a child of God must think and reason according to the Word of God. This can only be achieved through knowing and internalizing what the word says about life's circumstances.

To put on the breastplate of righteousness, there has to be daily meditation on the Word of God, the hearing of the preacher, discussions of the word and a deep desire to know the will of God. The scripture bids us to set our affections on things above for it is only by doing this will we achieve anything desired.

Addictions do not just disappear. It takes a deliberate effort by the addict to avoid the object of the addiction. Addictions at their worst are deep-seated and require warfare and deliverance. If ones addictions seem to be overtaking one then there is need to seek God in prayer and fasting who will give you direction if you really have the mind to overcome. If you know you need to overcome but cannot find the strength to do so, ask for help. Confess your faults to a trusted saint and get help to work on this problem. You will have someone to stand in the gap and cover you spiritually from any attacks until you achieve spiritual freedom to fight back. You however cannot say you want to overcome and still meddle in the addictive practice or its appetizers.

Illustration

If for example you are addicted to alcoholic beverages, then you will need to avoid all alcoholic products. No matter how small the concentration of alcohol is in that product for it is whetting that appetite. Many believers are addicted to pornography. It is said that originally this type of material was compiled to glorify a Greek goddess of sexual immorality. When a believer therefore views pornography, he or she puts him or herself in a position of glorifying this goddess. One hoping to overcome such an addiction cannot then claim to be doing a research on the types of such materials or just browsing through to suit curiosity. Looking at the television with squinted eyes does not make it any less of a sin. Neither can one who is striving to overcome a Spirit of fornication constantly put him or herself in a private place or in private conversations with the opposite sex. This is just a covert way of whetting the appetite.

Starving the addiction

What the addict has to do is to avoid ALL things associated with the addiction as best as he or she can. The main object of the addiction has to be forsaken so that healing can take place. Some persons have even gone as far as to avoid watching the television for a period of time if their addiction is so related. This can be a huge sacrifice but it is worth the saving of your soul. After all the Bible says if your right hand offends you, cut it off. For it is better to enter heaven maimed than to enter hell with both hands. Stifling the addiction may cause one to lose certain associates. This is a good thing though it may hurt. It is good because whenever God is cleaning out an area of our life, He also distances the people who contribute to the mess.

Sometimes the object of the addiction is unavoidable as it is in our regular working, home or church environment. What does the addict do in such a case? There is only one thing to do, internalize the Word of God and change the thinking, "for a young man can only cleanse his ways by taking heed to the word of God…." (Psalm 119:9). This is where the breastplate comes in. when one exposes himself to the transforming power of the Word of God, it becomes easy to resist the Devil and when he is resisted, he has no other option but to flee.

The Memories

In overcoming an addiction, the thoughts of the "good" experiences you have had with the issue of the addiction will play over in your mind. What you have to do is counter these thoughts with the thoughts of God. Remember what Paul said in his letter to the Philippians, "Finally, brothers, whatever things are true, whatever things are honest, whatever things are just, whatever things are pure, whatever things are lovely, whatever things are of good report; if there be any virtue, and if there be any praise, think on these things" (Philippians 4:8). You therefore need to speak to your mind on this issue.

The enemy will also fight back to maintain his strong hold but just remember that if you resist the Devil then he will flee and it is with the mind that we serve the Lord so we have to keep our minds pure. It is also useful to look at the postpaid benefits. In the future, sin pays death while righteousness, later pays life. Which is better to live for? One will work at a job which has the best retirement benefits so we should live the life which will provide the best eternal pay out. What now is being enjoyed in time is trivial because we are eternal creatures who are merely occupying time and waiting for eternity. We then should not dwell on things that satisfy in this life only, but we should live for the eternal splendor to which no earthly pleasure can ever be compared. After all, the Lord says that no matter how high our imagination is of the splendors of heaven, it is still greater than that, (paraphrased) I Corinthians 2:9.

Hopelessness

In overcoming an addiction sometimes it feels hopeless. It often feels as though the addiction is going to overtake you or consume you. Even after you have surrendered it into the hands of the Lord, the Devil still pushes and pressures you into believing that you will lose. I dare to tell you at this point that God has never failed in a situation that has been delivered to Him. Baby Samuel, the weak and cowardly Gideon; slow of speech Moses; drunken Noah; singing Jehoshaphat; nervous Hezekiah; scared Elijah. Greater is He that is in you than he that is in the world. No weapon formed against you shall prosper. As I write this section, I have attained the relevant experience that testifies to the Power of God over an addiction.

Anecdote

I had been overtaken by an addiction for a number of months. I had asked the Lord to take it away from me but as soon as it seemed to have vanished, there came an inner inclination that started it up again. I had tried all I knew but did not seem to be winning. One night in church I spoke to the Lord and told him that I knew that He would never fail when a situation was turned over to Him. I also told him that he could prove himself to me, by helping me to overcome my addiction. I surrendered it again into His hand and told Him that I was out of ideas. That very night, my addiction confronted me in my dream. The victory was realized in the morning when I awoke because my best friend and prayer partner had excellent news for me. She said that in her dream, a demon entered a big white room where she and I were and I hid behind her as she aggressively rebuked the demon until he backed out through the door. Little did she know that God had used her to overcome the demon of my addiction. I rejoiced in my heart and for the first time in many months I was truly free. God is faithful. This is the power of having a prayer partner.

If you ever become addicted, you need to seek to be prayed for because a slave is hardly able to have dominion over his master except by external powers. As a matter of fact, slaves in Egypt were subject to their masters in every way and even their unborn child belonged to the dominion of the master. Remember that whatever you are addicted to becomes your master. One therefore needs the help of the Holy Spirit so as to be empowered to overcome. The prayer of faithful saints can stir God to supply this power.

You may be wondering how to surrender the addiction to Jesus. It is really simple. Decide in your heart that you are tired of failing in this area of your life and let Him know that you do not know the way by yourself.

One song writer said- "I surrender all". Surrendering all means your life, your decisions, your direction, your struggles and all other things related to your life. Jesus is our saviour and wants to save us from every area of life that hampers our spiritual growth.

Chapter Four

The wile of Fear

Fear can be found on the opposite side of the spectrum to the most fundamental part of Christianity- faith. Fear is lit by lack of knowledge and then fueled by a lack of understanding. The Bible says of this wile of fear that it is not a part of God's package for the believer. "For God has not given us the Spirit of fear; but of power, and of love, and of a sound mind..." (II Timothy 1:7). This fear has to do with the fear of forces outside of the work of God towards the saving of our souls.

> Fear is far opposite to the Christian
> essential of faith

There is however a positivity to fear as when we are admonished to fear God and keep his commandments. "Let us hear the conclusion of the whole matter: Fear God, and keep his commandments: for this is the whole duty of man" (Ecclesiastes 12:13). This means reverential trust and Awe but not terror. What we will be looking at however is how the enemy has tried to counter the effects of faith in order to cripple the power of God in our lives; his keynote tool being FEAR.

When one fears a tactic or strategy of the enemy or the enemy himself, one fails to acknowledge the omniscience of God. God has already declared that "Ye are of God, little children, and have overcome them: because greater is he that is in you, than he that is in the world" (I John 4:4). The

God who knows all things all the time says that we are greater in power than our enemy but yet we fear.

> The God who knows all things all the time says that
> we are greater in power than our enemy

When the enemy attacks us it is not that he knows he can win but that he hopes that he can inject us with enough fear so that the power of God cannot move in our lives; Bearing in mind that all things are accomplished through faith. On our own, the enemy has victory over us because we were for many years servants to sin. We were servants to the Devil because we did not possess the power to overcome him or to redeem ourselves. However, when the Spirit of God, who banished Satan from heaven, came into us, we became empowered to win in ALL battles over our enemies. This is so true but we can only be powerful and effective if we believe the Word of God. "But without faith it is impossible to please him: for he that comes to God must believe that he is, and that he is a rewarder of them that diligently seek him" (Hebrews 11:6). We therefore have to take God at his word in order for our Spiritual abilities to be activated.

Of course it is known that it takes special Spiritual alertness to counter the enemy in certain dimensions. After all, the Bible teaches that "… we wrestle not against flesh and blood, but against principalities, against powers, against the rulers of the darkness of this world, against Spiritual wickedness in high places" (Ephesians 6:12). The Devil knows that if he gets us into a corner cringing from fear then the power of God, which comes through belief in his word, will not be activated. Therefore, in order to get the victory over us each time, the Devil injects a dose of fear and watches it as it works on us. Let us go practical with this.

Have you ever been so afraid of something that you deprived yourself of sleep? Well, I have been in such a situation. I will start this section with a personal experience.

Anecdote

When I first got saved, I realized something unusual was happening to me. Sometimes when I went to sleep my Spirit would separate from my body and just be suspended in mid air. At these times I could not awake even though I always wanted to. I was always scared and would fight to get back into my body. A few months later I realized that whenever I was sleeping and another Spirit entered the room then my Spirit would again separate from my body and I could observe the physical movements in the room as though I were wide awake. I would panic and try to call out to someone in the house but it was as though no sound came out of me. Often I would have to relax to get back into my body and I would pray that I would never see the other Spirit that was there in the room. I was often afraid to sleep especially when I was alone at home.

As I grew in the grace of God the activities got more intense. I remember one afternoon as I lie in bed at home and dozed off, a strange presence entered the room. My Spirit at once exited my body and observed. I could see the demon this time in the form of a monkey. At that very moment my cellular telephone on the bed alerted me that a text message had just arrived. I tried to get to the phone but my Spirit slipped through it each time so I left it; as I watched the demon on the window. I was filled with fear and just thought- 'I am so dead' (I gave up out of fear). At that very instant, my Spirit fell back into my body and I was wide awake in the room. I checked my phone for the text message and realized that a text had indeed come in a few minutes earlier. I was so afraid that I vouched never to sleep on that section of the bed at that time of the day again. I never wanted to be home alone thereafter because I was filled with fear.

About six months later it was revealed to me that whenever an evil Spirit came around, then my Spirit exited my body so that it could rage a Spiritual warfare- Spirit to Spirit. I was so sad thinking that I had spent so much time in fear because I lacked understanding. This is truly the reason the scripture says that in all our getting we should get understanding as expressed in Proverbs 4:7. After I got this understanding, I prayed for another of those Spiritual experiences so that I could stand up to my enemy. I knew this rematch was a must because that is a way of God- He allows us a second chance to win in our very place of past defeats. It was almost 3 months later while I vacationed on the Island of Curacao in the Netherland Antilles that I got my break through.

> God allows us a second chance to win in our very
> place of past defeats

41

I was sleeping in a family size guest room that I was sharing with three other family members when I was alerted to the presence of a demon in the room. My Spirit picked him up and I observed him carefully. The demon was in three parts but it was one Spirit. The first section was a whole dark shadow lying on one of the beds. The second was a section of the body from the waist downwards. The portion of this Spirit which took note of me however was the third part. This section was the torso which was suspended in front of the standing fan in the room.

I started to speak the word of faith, pleading the blood of Jesus but the demon seemed stubborn and I found that I started to say-"I strangle the plans of the adversary in the name of Jesus." I watched the demon as his neck got smaller and smaller as though the very words from my mouth were strangling him until finally his head just spun out into the fan and disappeared. I had won! I got up that morning feeling empowered.

When I got back home to Jamaica a few days later, I declared to a church sister that I am no longer fearful of demons but they must now be fearful of me. That night in service a preacher proclaimed-"that which you once feared is now afraid of you". My victory was confirmed and I am more than a conqueror.

That was 5 months ago from this present moment of writing and I have not had another encounter with those Spirits. I am however on my guard because I know that the enemy left Jesus only for a season and so he will come at me again. I know that faith in God can move mountains and make us free indeed.

Fear is meant to be crippling, deafening and blinding but God gives the victory.

> Fear is meant to paralyze us but God gives the victory

Part II

Why DO WE fear SO READILY?

From we were infants; we were exposed to certain experiences which taught us to fear. We knew that the people around us could not always protect us from the school bully, the bad dog in the neighborhood or the scary black heart man who could show up at anytime to kidnap us. We simply learnt that we had to fear, at least sometimes.

Many times we have had our close friends and parents fail us. We have learnt the hard way, the very fact that the arm of flesh shall fail. We have also heard of others who have had horrible experiences that we fear could happen to us. For example, we hear daily of persons being kidnapped and killed, we therefore avoid being by ourselves walking anywhere at nights. A simple act of seeing someone accidentally drop something from his hands can evoke fear in us. With all these expectations and experiences, Christianity seemingly presents a problem to our minds.

The Great problem

When we begin our walk with the Lord Jesus Christ, he presents a package which includes comprehensive security. One says that experience teaches wisdom and so with all the negative experiences which warrant fear, it becomes very difficult for us to just take up this new security. We get held back because we do not wait on God to prove himself faithful. Instead of waiting and being of good courage, we start acting according to our fears. One knows that if a person claims to be something then the logical thing to do is to allow him to demonstrate his claim when the situation arises. However, when our lives are at stake, logics are replaced by impulses. This mentality usually disrupts the plan of God and prevents us from learning a lesson of faith and security. God therefore puts us in the same situation over and over again to teach us but we fear and take a long time to learn.

> Christ provides complete security

Even after we have come to the knowledge of the Lord and savior Jesus Christ, fear can still grip us. Often times we do not move according to the will of God and then we fear that God will not be faithful. This is a reasonable position because if we do not stand on good grounds with our master, we are at his mercy rather than his favour. Even though God cannot do but be faithful, we still are affected in this regard. Can a blind man walk confidently, without a stick or a dog or someone else to guide him? No. So we become spiritually lost when we deviate from the will of God and try things our own way. We are prone to stumble and our very Spirit knows this and fears.

> If we do not stand on good grounds with our master, we are at his mercy rather than his favour.

Knowledge, whether true or false also contributes to our fears. If, for example, we are taught that God will not hear our prayer if we only cry to him when we are in need, then this can be dangerous if we believe such. (Even though it is not a practice that pleases God), a teaching of this nature can cause a struggling Christian to lose faith and Hope. We therefore have to ensure that the teachings that we accept, all line up with the Word of God and are taught in the proper context. It is known that God would never contradict himself and that the Bible is the basis of all absolute truth.

Part III

How to KILL Fear

As on the colour wheel, the only perfect contrast for a colour is the one directly opposite to it and so the only true remedy for fear is FAITH. Faith in God and in the power of his might is the way out. "So then faith comes by hearing, and hearing by the word of God" (Romans 10:17). It is therefore through hearing and believing the Word of God that fear is crippled and ultimately killed in our lives. We see that one of the stipulated conditions for a man not to go to war is if he is fearful according to Deuteronomy 20:8. It is known that a man who is fearful in mind is one who has already conceived in his thoughts that the chances of losing far supersede the chances of winning. Why then would one so faint hearted be brought into battle?

Illustrated

Joshua was admonished to 'fear not'. He then encouraged the people to 'fear not'. This is so because a battle is won in faith. The reason Jehovah told Joshua to fear not and gave him the discourse in Joshua 1:1- 9 was to build his faith. It was indeed the word from God himself that gave Joshua the faith and courage to go on. A word received from the Lord can be totally relied on because God is not a man that he should lie. The scriptures are the words of God from which he directs the affairs of his people- the church. God is said to honour his word above his name. Therefore, whatever he says that he will do. The words of the Lord are ye and ye and Amen.

There are scriptures for every battle situation in the life of the believer. Once our lives are aligned with the words of God, there are some victories that are assured us. Firstly, "when the enemy shall come in like a flood, the Spirit of the LORD shall lift up a standard against him" (Isaiah 59:19). This simply means that no matter how overwhelming the enemy seems to get, even when he puts forth his best to destroy us, God has a standard that he will raise up that will protect and preserve us.

Next is Psalm 91:7 which states that- "A thousand shall fall at your side, and ten thousand at your right hand; but it shall not come near you." This clearly depicts a supernatural protection. No matter how many persons around you seem to be failing and dying without a hope, God has made provision for your protection. Look at how many babies died around baby Moses and baby Jesus yet they perished not. Even in the event of natural armed forces coming upon us, it is known that "The angel of the LORD encamps round about them that fear him, and delivers them" (Psalm 34:7). This is demonstrated in the story of David and King Saul as presented in II Samuels 23:26-28.

> "And Saul went on this side of the mountain, and David and his men on that side of the mountain: and David made haste to get away for fear of Saul; for Saul and his men compassed David and his men round about to take them. But there came a messenger unto Saul, saying, Haste thee, and come; for the Philistines have made a raid upon the land. So Saul returned from pursuing after David, and went against the Philistines: therefore they called that place Sela–hammahlekoth."

We clearly see how the Lord delivered when there seemed to have been no way. This is the very strength of God. He specializes in the seemingly impossible. The enemy will not triumph over us unless we lay ourselves carelessly. The story rendered of Rehab the harlot depicts a key principle. After we embrace faith, we must also act in faith.

When rehab hid the spies she was promised safety when Israel came to take over Jericho. However, there was a condition that Rehab had to abide by. She had to ensure that all her family members remained in her house. Once they were in the house, the armies of Israel were responsible to ensure their protection. However, if anyone left the house, which is the covering, then he would be in direct danger of annihilation. We have no need to fear once we are staying under the blood of Jesus. The blood is the tower, the defense and the fortress. Outside of the blood are dangerous grounds. To overcome fear, we therefore have to make a concerted effort to remain in right standing with God which gives him no other option but to be faithful to his word.

We as believers are also hedged about. The enemy cannot come near us unless he is permitted to do so. We are safe and secure in the protected city of God which is watched by prophets who are chosen by God. The city is fortified by the prayers of the saints and kept nourished through praise and worship.

Be Prepared

Preparation is also a preventative measure to fear. Arm yourself with the Word of God and be ready to cut the Devil with it. After all, it is the only offensive weapon of the warfare. In Ephesians6: 12-17 we see where all the weapons to use against the enemy are used to defend from blows or attacks however, the Word is the only one we can use to return a blow.

"For our wrestling is not against flesh and blood, but against the principalities, against the powers, against the world–rulers of this darkness, against the Spiritual hosts of wickedness in the heavenly places. Wherefore take up the whole armour of God that ye may be able to withstand in the evil day, and, having done all, to stand. Stand therefore, having girded your loins with truth, and having put on the breastplate of righteousness, and having shod your feet with the preparation of the gospel of peace; withal taking up the shield of faith, wherewith ye shall be able to quench all the fiery darts of the evil one. And take the helmet of salvation, and the sword of the Spirit, which is the word of God" (Ephesians 6: 12).

We must therefore be armed with the word because if we go to war with only shield and helmet and only tools meant to protect us from a blow then the enemy will flea uninjured out of frustration. This means he will return in a short while after. However, if we have a weapon to throw blows at the enemy then we will surely do some damage and have a longer period of rest.

A soldier is also more confident in the battle when he has proven his tools. This was the reason David refused the armoury that King Saul provided for the battle against Goliath. David preferred the sling and stones which he was skilled at using rather than some fancy equipment. We therefore need to exercise using our tools so that when the war rages we can boldly apply the correct piece of tool for the correct blow.

Fear, being a Spiritual weapon, can be very devastating. One may find that it takes more than just a word to cast fear away especially when the fear itself is not found in you but in one who is weaker spiritually than you are. Let me hasten to tell you another testimony.

Anecdote

A new member of our church family shared a testimony of faith with us. He said that his wife had been literally crippled by fear for months. She could not walk at all because fear had gripped her heart and made her unable to use her limbs. He said for all this time he had to take care of her as well as his children. He recounted that one morning as he was praying, his Spirit exited his body and he could see himself kneeling in prayer. He said that his Spirit looked around only to see his wife moving through the passage towards him with a kitchen knife. He immediately awakened from the vision and he looked around to see if his wife was indeed behind him but she was not.

He reported that he ran to the living room couch where she spent most of her days. There he found her with her eyes tightly shut and her head moving from side to side. He called her by name and asked her what was wrong. She said to him that the Devil was telling her to kill him, their children and then herself. This brother said that he decided that enough was enough. He got into some instant prayer and commanded the Devil to take his flight. He said that it was in his praying that he saw a demon around the side of his house with a bucket filled with slime and all manner of messy things. The demon was about to empty the bucket in his yard and he commanded it not to do so. The demon then emptied the bucket over the fence. The brother reported that in that same hour his wife sprang off the couch and began rejoicing in the God of their salvation.

This incident shows that by ourselves we cannot overcome the darts thrown at us but with God, and through God, we can do valiantly. Fear has nothing over us once we are armed with the word which is Spirit and life.

Chapter Five

The wile of 'The cares of life'

Who is not bombarded with the cares of life? For the average human being there is so much to do and to contemplate. Wake up early; prepare breakfast; get to work or school on time; ensure that outstanding projects are going according to deadlines; make lunch arrangements; personal development and oops, get the kids' or your parents' health and life insurance; get them clothes and food. Check on the investments, pay mortgage and student loans but do not forget the utility bills which are coming one after the other. Be early for church service but before others get there; ensure that you are prepared to lead or follow the leading of God. It's night again. Iron for the morning's activities, ensure that breakfast items are in place and do not forget to clean up the dinner dishes in the sink. Just in time, the daily newspaper is to be read and since crime is on the upsurge you have to seek better security for the property- so that is also on your mind.

> There is always something to care about

Many persons have these things to deal with daily and others have more things that could be added to this list but do you realize that these activities almost effortlessly squeeze out God? Yes, that is the aim. The Devil knows that if he applies the pressure to us then he gets us almost too busy to even breathe a prayer. There was a movie released some years ago which revealed that women are almost always thinking a secondary thought while they are carrying out a primary action. If this is so for most human beings, then along with that list of tasks outlined earlier, the mind would be ladened with an extremely heavy burden. The Devil maximizes on this weakness in a cunning way.

In operation, God works on our desires and also gives us the desires of our hearts. "Delight yourself also in the LORD: and he shall give you the desires of your heart" (Psalms 37:4). "For it is God which works in you both to will and to do of his good pleasure" (Philippians 2:13). Our heart in this context is synonymous to our mind. The writer in Colossians 3:2 admonishes us to set our affections on things above. This is so because whatever we set our minds on, then that is what we are shaping up to become. This therefore means that when the Devil gets us too busy to have heavenly priorities then we are basically missing our heavenly appointments.

> Whatever we set our minds on, we will become

The promises of God are ye and ye and amen but these promises must be released through prayer. This principle was demonstrated in Babylon as Israel served the full sentence of their captivity- 70 years. No freedom began until Daniel realized and started to pray. How can we request something or seek it earnestly if we do not even have the desire for it? One knows that one first has to set the mind on a thing before one can truly get the drive to pursue it. We first have to catch the vision in the mind then the Holy Ghost starts his resolve to bring it to pass.

God says "behold I stand at the door and knock; if any man hears my voice and open the door, I will come in to him, and sup with him, and he with me" (Revelations 3:20). God does not force his way in, but rather allows us the choice. Therefore if our minds are too crowded, then we will not even hear the knocking.

> How can we request something or seek it earnestly if we do not even have the desire for?

"For as he thinketh in his heart, so is he" (Proverbs 23:7) is a scripture quoted very frequently. This is a stark reality since it has been proven that one who is motivated achieves greatness because his heart believes and is set on achieving. We become our thoughts.

> As a man thinketh in his heart, so is he

In the story of Saul and David we see the thought of envy in Saul towards David materializing into a hunt for the young lad's life. Saul, thought it, focused on it, worked towards it and became it- a murderer not of David but because of his hatred for David. Saul perfected his intent to kill that he slayed the priests of God.

To this same degree, Christians are admonished to set their affections on things above. This will make earthly responsibilities easier and make heavenly choices easier to make. Such a shift takes away cares from us.

> Set your affections on God not on your cares. He cares for your cares

Part II

Why are we so vulnerable to the cares of life?

'The cares of life', is a perfect wile because it is one to which all human beings are vulnerable. The book of Job clearly states it this way- "Man that is born of a woman is of few days and full of trouble" (Job 14:1). We all have cares of some kind.

The Devil does not even have to create the cares because they are already there so all he does is exaggerate the importance or enormity of them. "Sufficient unto the day is the evil thereof…" (St. Matthew 6:34), is another well known scripture.

> Man that is born of a woman is of a few days and full of trouble

However we take thought of weeks, months and even years. As humans, we tend to feel that we are responsible to take care. This sense of responsibility heightens especially when we become the head of a home or of some other group.

The cares of life present themselves in every aspect of life; from simple things such as buying the supplies for school to paying the bills and fees. We are vulnerable because it is almost second nature to try to figure out solutions to every problem. The system of the world is that of a problem-solving approach to everything. We therefore start believing that we have to and are obligated to but most dangerously we believe that we can solve all the issues that life presents. The very sinner's life testifies to this inability. They usually say that they will fix their lives and then come to Christ but seldom come because they cannot achieve this prerequisite. We can never fix our lives and neither do we have to for the Lord provides the perfect model.

> We can never fix our lives and neither do we have to because God provides the perfect model

Part III

How to deal with the cares of life?

Among the pieces of armor in the book of Ephesians, we are encouraged to put on the helmet of salvation. This is a head piece that has to do with the mind. We are also admonished to gird up the loins of our mind and be sober. The helmet of salvation indicates that we be acquainted with the contents of the salvation package and that our minds and thought processes be saturated with same. One chief component of this package is the coverage of 'cares'.

> The helmet of salvation indicates a mind saturated with the package of salvation

To deal with cares, the helmet of salvation dictates that which is said in I Peter 5:7- "Casting all your cares on him; for he cares for you." The first time I really experienced this scripture in my life was the period in which I sought a job. Having sent out a few applications, I realized that no calls were coming in. I got worried but when I almost broke down, the scripture, quoted above ministered to me. I then realized that the Lord knew my cares and that he was ready to solve them if I only cast them on him.

> God deals with our cares when we cast them on him

Illustration

When the Lord asked Philip 'how they were going to feed the multitude', the scripture reports the following "When Jesus then lifted up his eyes, and saw a great company come to him, he said to Philip, From where shall we buy bread, that these may eat? And this he said to prove him: for he himself knew what he would do. Philip answered him, Two hundred pennyworth of bread is not sufficient for them, that every one of them may take a little" (St. John 6:5-7). This proves that though it may seem as if you are left to find the way out, Jesus already knows the solution. He already has a plan.

> Though God puts a question to us, he already has a plan

When the Angel, in Revelations 5:2 asked John "who shall open the books?" it was no problem that John could not find a man because God was already the HOW. Jesus Christ is the care taker. He has all the answers.

The issue of worry is one that is settled in scriptures. The bible encourages us through the person of Christ not to worry about tomorrow.

"Therefore I say to you, Take no thought for your life, what you shall eat, or what you shall drink; nor yet for your body, what shall you put on. Is not the life more than meat, and the body than raiment? Behold the fowls of the air: for they sow not, neither do they reap, nor gather into barns; yet your heavenly Father feeds them. Are you not much better than they? Which of you by taking thought can add one cubit to his stature? And why take you thought for raiment? Consider the lilies of the field, how they grow; they toil not, neither do they spin: And yet I say to you, that even Solomon in all his glory was not arrayed like one of these. Why, if God so clothe the grass of the field, which today is, and tomorrow is cast into the oven, shall he not much more clothe you, O you of little faith? Therefore take no thought, saying, what shall we eat? Or, what shall we drink? Or, Wherewithal shall we be clothed?(For after all these things do the Gentiles seek) for your heavenly Father knows that you have need of all these things. But seek you first the kingdom of God, and his righteousness; and all these things shall be added to you. Take therefore no thought for the morrow: for the morrow shall take thought for the things of itself. Sufficient to the day is the evil thereof" (St. Matthew 6: 25-34).

This clearly teaches that there is no room for worrying because many things that we worry about never happen. What then is the profit if we worry when it will not add to us the thing that we worry for? If God takes thought for sparrows and lilies and grass which have no soul, how much more will he care for man whom he gave his life for? We are so valuable to him that when we become his children, we become the sheep of his pastures. This thought means that we are the reason he makes provisions. So then if God makes provisions because of us, will he not give it to us freely? We are the children of the righteous and David said that "… I have not seen the righteous forsaken, nor his seed begging bread" (Psalm 37:25).

> Worry does not add but rather takes from us that which we have

The scripture also clearly teaches that "…no good thing shall he withhold from them that walk uprightly" (Psalm 84:11). Also, if we delight ourselves in Him then he will give us the desires of our heart. This simply means that we just have to care about the Kingdom business while we cast all other cares on him and he will see us through.

Illustration

When a person joins the military of a country, in essence what the government says is- 'we will feed you, clothe you and take care of your cares, only serve us'. This is exactly what the LORD says to us- the soldiers of his army. Delight yourself in my work, seek ye first my kingdom and I will supply all your need but most importantly, I am your Commander-your shepherd, so you shall not even want.

Anecdote

There was a discussion some years ago in a Christian youth forum about 'God's coming through for us'. A question was asked- 'Does God always comes through for us?' Answers were given in the negative and in the affirmative and were both correct. The reasoning was simply this- if we see 'coming through' as getting the answer we want then God does not always 'come through'. However if we see 'coming through' in the right sense which is - getting the result that is best for us, then God always come through. Simply said- if God does not give it to us then it is not good for us. How so you might ask? However, he promises that no good thing shall he withhold from them that walk uprightly.

Another thing to consider is an analogy I stumbled across a few years ago. It is said that keeping our cares while accepting Christ is like one who is walking down a lonely desert track with a heavy load on his back. A good Samaritan appears from over the hills driving a Land Rover, though old and worn. He stops and offers you a ride and you hop in with your load. You are asked why you keep your bag pack on. Out of consideration and gratitude you share that- it is already a great deal that the Samaritan has given you a ride therefore you do not want to give him the added job of carrying your load also. In response he says- but I'm already carrying the load so take it off and leave it in my total care.

> Why would we want to carry our cares that
> Christ has opted to carry for us?

Applied

God gives us the desires of our hearts

I will share another of my experiences which shaped my writing. While I boiled with zeal for the things of God and for God, He taught me this principle. One evening while I was back in College one of my colleagues asked me to hold a bag for her. I got curious as I came to realize that it was a gift item. I peeked into the bag to see a beautiful watch set with replaceable bands. These bands were many– about 12 in number and of all different colours. The set also contained watch faces of gold and silver and other types of metal alloys. I hastily shut the bag and hoped that this gift was mine. However it was not and I soon forgot about this watch set.

A few months later when I went home, one of my relatives saw me about 3 months before my birthday and asked me what was my desired birthday gift. Before I could respond she told me to think about it and so I agreed. One night about a month after that incident, I went to a church service many miles away and returned home very late that night. I saw a strange box on my bed and I asked my mother why it was there. She said it was my godmother who had sent me an early birthday gift. When I opened the box, lo and behold it was the same watch set that I had secretly desired for a few minutes, some months before.

The very thing happened to me several times after to confirm that it was a lesson from God. It was an expression of his love. Just to lift your faith undoubtedly I will share another experience. As I yearned one evening for some evening dresses, a long lost cousin from America called five minutes following my thought to say that she had just bought some evening dresses for me. Of course she may not have bought them in that same hour but the very incident proved to me that God knows my desires afar off and will stick to his promise if I just cast my cares on him.

More applications

Another day while I was leaving work, I saw one of my colleagues in a beautiful pair of shoes. It was the first time that I had seen any of that sort and I admired it. It is said that there is an element of desire in admiration so I perhaps desired it too. That weekend as I visited my mother to collect some things that had arrived for me from America, something awesome happened. My mother said, referring to a pair of shoes, 'this also came but I don't know if you would want it.' I squirmed with excitement because it was that very pair of shoes that I had seen and admired a few days earlier. If that were not enough, my colleague with the shoes called my attention to the fact that they were the same brand of shoes and were made in the same place. God is amazing.

Something to remember is that though the cares of life are many, the provisions of God are greater than these all.

> If God does not give it to us, then it is not good for us

Final analysis

When the cares of life overtake you, simply get so focused on the things of God that they grow dim and watch God take care of you. It is simple and easy. Ensure that you put your day together in such a way that nothing interrupts your God time and keep it like this. Pretty soon one day will become eternity and all the cares will pass away.

> The cares of life are the Devil's distracters. Put them away into the hands of God and live on with life

Chapter six

The wile of DESPAIR

The very essence of the gospel of the Lord Jesus Christ is to provide hope for a people who were a 'brand to the burning'. This means a people that were born to die without a hope. The Lord came to make a way of escape for us from the death sentence of sin. We were heading towards an inevitable doom and this was reason enough for despair.

However the born again believer has no reason to feel or entertain this emotion. The hope presented by Christ is an eternal one. The hope in Christ is intended to comfort us as we wait for the return of the redeemer and friend.

> Christ gives the born again believer Hope which should cast away despair

There was a tradition among the Jews concerning men of great wealth who went to the market to buy. If he saw an animal or any other possession that he wanted, he would move towards attaining it. If he realized then that he did not possess the space to sustain the animal or the item of purchase on his property then he would pay for it and seals it with his signet from his ring. He would then leave it in the marketplace and go home to make preparation for the item. As soon as the preparation was made, he would return to redeem his purchase.

> "I go to prepare a place for you …. I will return
> and take you unto myself" (St. John 14:2).

How beautifully this fits what the Lord has done for us. He came for a people who rejected him and so he sealed, by his Spirit, others who were available. Now he is gone to prepare a place for his purchased ones so that he can one day return to receive his bride. Let me prove this:

Purchased with the blood of Christ "For as much as you know that you were not redeemed with corruptible things, as silver and gold, from your vain conversation received by tradition from your fathers; But with the precious blood of Christ, as of a lamb without blemish and without spot" (I Peter 1:18).

Sealed by the Holy Spirit "…and grieve not the Holy Spirit of God, whereby you are sealed to the day of redemption" (Ephesians 4:30).

Gone to prepare a place to return again. "Let not your heart be troubled: you believe in God, believe also in me. In my Father's house are many mansions: if it were not so, I would have told you. I go to prepare a place for you. And if I go and prepare a place for you, I will come again, and receive you to myself; that where I am, there you may be also" (St. John 14:1).

Therefore, seeing that our father is gone only for a while then we can wait with joy knowing that now is our salvation nearer that when we first believed. Better is indeed awaiting us. There is a confidence that the Lord affords those who trust in him. There is a peace that belongs to those who embrace this confidence and there is a joy in knowing that the actions of God are directed toward your better end.

Despair is a tool of craftiness. The device of despair is meant to counteract the hope that the Christian has in the Lord Jesus Christ. Despair is intended to cancel the effect of the promises of God. Therefore if one accepts despair then he calls God a liar. The gospel is not about feelings but rather about knowing. It is all in the mind and so the writer bids us to be transformed by the renewing of our minds. The emotion of happiness is altered by feelings but hope shall not be moved. The Christian journey is such that there are many ups and downs which are the tools God uses to bring us to perfect gold. He knows the path I take and when I come out I shall be as pure gold.

If life were on one plain, a mountain experience would not be regarded as such, and neither would we know the way of the valley. The enemy maximizes on the valley experiences of many believers by pressuring them into believing that God has somehow forgotten them. The question is really, can God forget?

Part II

Why are we so apt to despair?

When we came to Christ, we were rugged and undone; overwhelmed by bad habits and sensual desires. We were overrun by a lack of hope as life worldly routine had us battered. We were accustomed to a system in which human love soon waxed cold after a few mistakes on our part. It was understandably the norm for someone to abandon us after we got five or six chances at making the same error.

When we got saved, a whole new system confronted us; That of abundant grace and mercies; Grace which could not easily be exhausted by any measure of human failure. A kindness and forgiveness that was far greater than seventy times seven; A system of exceedingly rich longsuffering; One that offered forgiveness for even that for which we could not forgive ourselves. This is where the challenge begins. The enemy wishes us to believe that some things are beyond forgiveness even though the scripture only names one unpardonable sin. Satan tries to inculcate in us that we can commit a sin once too many and that we can exhaust the grace of God.

While this is true of presumptuous sin, one must realize that once there is a beckoning to repent then it is the urging of the Lord since we have no good desires in ourselves. It was the apostle Paul who said in Philippians 2:13 "For it is God which works in you both to will and to do of his good pleasure." Hence the very will in us is the move and continued working of the Lord on our hearts.

> Once there is a beckoning to repent then it is the urging of the Lord since we have no good desires in ourselves

We despair easily because we are accustomed to broken promises then apologies and new promises from our parents, friends or spouses. However, God is not a man that he should lie so whatever he says he will do, he will, because he has all power in His hands. We fail to remember that all the unconditional promises were made with God's foreknowledge of all that we would have done. This we fail to hold on to therefore when God takes more than the time we designated to him, we take it that he has forfeited and somehow changed His mind.

> All the unconditional promises were made with God's foreknowledge of all that we would have done this did not prevent him from making these promises

We despair because we do not understand the ways of God. "For as the heavens are higher than the earth, so are my ways higher than your ways, and my thoughts than your thoughts" (Isaiah 55:9). God does not exist for the use of man but rather, man for God. For had there been no God, there would be no man. However, if there were no man, God would still stand as He did before the beginning.

Anecdote

As I prepared this chapter a recent experience came to mind. One day I felt great despair as the Devil tried to oppress me. I said to the lord that 'after all that I had done in disobedience to him that I did not think that he would continue to work with me'. He sent the scripture- "my thoughts are not your thoughts neither are my ways your ways saith the Lord." This was a word of both rebuke and comfort. There is none like God.

The way God does his thing is better understood in its end for we cannot accurately estimate it even if it involves the same people, the same time, same situation and the same need. For God specializes in doing the same thing many different times in many different ways.

> Who can by searching find out God?

Part III

How to counter the wile of despair?

Firstly feeling low or forsaken does not necessarily mean that the Lord has deserted you. You are the prized possession for which the savior has already made the most expensive payment: His blood. He was willing to do whatsoever was required to save your soul and that he did. If you were the only person on the earth, the savior would still have died, just as how Adam being the only man, God met with him in the cool of the evening; always.

> GOD was willing to do whatsoever it would have taken to save YOUR soul

If God wanted you to fail then he would have left you in the world where you were actually doing just that. God is not cruel to call you out of darkness to watch you cringe and fail. Also, whatever you are going through is a direct working of God. "...and we know that all things work together for good to them that love God, to them who are the called according to his purpose" (Romans 8:28).

> If God wanted you to fail then he would have left you in the world where you were actually doing just that

How do you know whether or not you are called? No one can truly come to Christ unless he is called of the father. This is so because the enmity in our mind against the things of God was so great that it would take a greater than it to overcome it. This over comer is the Spirit of God that breaks the barrier and gives us a conviction from which hope springs. We can therefore rest assured that though we seem to be going through hell; whether self inflicted or divinely designed, God is still working His purpose through it. For when we would have completed this stage, we would have learnt valuable lessons.

Anecdote

I can recall after my conversion that one afternoon I thought to myself, 'how am I going to make it when so many people are failing?' The Spirit's overwhelming response to me was the word of St John 15: 16 which says- "You have not chosen me, but I have chosen you, and ordained you, that you should go and bring forth fruit, and that your fruit should remain: that whatever you shall ask of the Father in my name, he may give it you." In that very moment I understood quite clearly that since God was the one who had chosen me then the way was already made by Him and that it was His business to see me through. One other thing that encouraged me in this regard was the fact that, as one preacher had said, "the Lord chose you because he saw in you the potential and ability to make it in the line of duty in which you are placed. Hence, it is not for you to worry but rather to just allow the Spirit to lead along the track that He has prepared for your particular train."

There was a period in my life when I just kept failing at obeying the voice of God. One morning as I was about to despair, the Spirit of the Lord spoke to me, "There is a victory in defeat". Within that same second, before I could ask what victory? The Spirit of God responded by saying- 'a more resolute mind'. It was indeed a fact for me. For each time I failed, my will to triumph got stronger until finally I got the strength to jump up, shake off the dust and run in patience.

Anecdote

Springing from such disobedient act which I know is a grave sin, I started to reason with God. I told him exactly how I felt. Sometimes I did not believe that he was going to work with me anymore because I felt that he was weary of me. It was then that he spoke the scripture that I earlier mentioned.

This simple thought made me feel so ashamed that I had thought so lowly of my merciful Lord but most importantly, it gave me hope far beyond that point of despair. It is for us to understand that the Lord looks at the heart of man. The desires and intention of your heart mean much to God. Though many of us fail, we do so with good intent or while trying very hard to stay on board. This causes the Lord, in his mercy to be longsuffering to us and to extend more grace to us until we stand firmly.

> God cares about your intentions. He looks at the heart

A feeling that God is not near can be very discouraging at times. When you have become particularly accustomed to the presence of God and then you seek him in his usual place and he cannot be found then it causes you to worry. There is an answer afforded us in scripture about this type of predicament.

"Behold, I go forward, but he is not there; and backward, but I cannot perceive him: On the left hand, where he does work, but I cannot behold him: he hides himself on the right hand, that I cannot see him: But he knows the way that I take: when he has tried me, I shall come forth as gold" (Job 23: 8).

In this situation, the righteous man Job could not find the Lord God. God had intentionally hid himself as he observed Job on his own. It is true that a good child behaves well in the presence of his parents but the real proof of the whole grooming is arrived at when the child is out of sight. Whenever God hides himself and you cannot sense his presence, it does not mean that he is not there but rather that he is observing you at your own leisure.

Furthermore, apart from a pain that affects the body of Christ, there is maybe one of three things happening whenever you feel low in your Spirit- a test, a trial or a temptation. A test is meant for the purpose of elevation; for in passing a test the tester sees that you have mastered that particular level. The Spirit realm is organized in ranks and this is how there are imps, demons, Devils, powers, principalities etc. As one is being tested, there may be a sense of frustration that God has once more allowed you to be confronted by that which you have been trying to avoid. However, the only way to totally overcome in the Spirit is to choose the way of God in the face of a much easier and Devilish way. One minister at my church often say- 'no test, then no testimony'

A test is intended to elevate you

On the other hand if you are passing through a trial, then it is intended to make you stronger. For when you are tried, your faith increases in God. One cannot know that God is a provider unless the trial of hunger and need reaches that one. Also, one cannot know that God is a healer unless sickness is allowed by the Holy Spirit. God works to make himself all things to his children and so he presents the trial to build us up. "…which is his body, the fullness of him that fills all in all" (Ephesians 1:23).

When we have a genuine need and we trust God to supply that need, then, when he does, our faith will be strengthened in that area, should that need re- cur. God will soon after present a greater need so that you can stretch your faith and grow from faith to faith. "For therein is the righteousness of God revealed from faith to faith: as it is written, the just shall live by faith" (Romans 1:17). God wants us to depend on him and so in learning to lean on Jesus, there has to be a trial for there to be a victory.

Trials are to make you strong

If the reason for your despair is overwhelming temptation then there is also a consolation in the Word of God. Firstly, the bible teaches that with every temptation comes a way of escape. It also teaches that whatever the temptation, it is common to man. " There has no temptation taken you but such as is common to man: but God is faithful, who will not suffer you to be tempted above that you are able; but will with the temptation also make a way to escape, that you may be able to bear it" (I Corinthians 10:13). There are some good things about temptations:- Temptations show us something remarkable. They teach us where our weak spots are.

A coward and well experienced opponent like the Devil would only hit us in our weak spot. Temptation is said to be as a result of lust and enticement. "But every man is tempted, when he is drawn away of his own lust, and entice" (James 1:14). Therefore, if I am tempted, it means that I have a mind or an eye on the object of the temptation. Think about it, you could not be tempted with cigarettes if you never thought of smoking or had a history of doing it. It would simply not be temptation. Therefore, when we are tempted, we see exactly where we need strength. What temptation does for us is also to present an opportunity for us to prove our love for God.

> Temptations show us where we need strength

The weak limb only gets strength through endurance exercises. I remember that I was complaining that whenever I sing from my diaphragm that my back would get totally weak as though I would fall. I told one of my co- workers who said the expected thing- "go to the gym and do some work on the muscles."

I have come to a place where I know that understanding of my situation can mean the difference between overcoming and dying. As I wrestled with the love of God one morning, I wondered in my Spirit if I really loved God or the things of God. I thought because I was so taken up with my theological studies, my writing and church duties that I was probably doing them for the wrong reason. I then questioned God. However, I knew that this was not a question from self but rather from God who wanted to clarify this matter in my Spirit. God has a way of showing us ourselves as we get closer to Him.

So, as the week went by and I prayed about this love affair, I realized that I had started to lose my appetite for the things of the Kingdom. Everything just tasted routinely boring and dull and to no end. It was a Sunday morning when it all reached its peak and I despaired that some clarity came. The Holy Spirit just chipped in to give me understanding that "God never intends to weary us" therefore, what I was going through was a process. I then remembered that I had asked God about my love for him. That was the moment in which I gained the understanding that God had made the Kingdom things dull so that I could measure my love for Him.

I went to church feeling much better. The word that came through that day was– "Lovest thou me more than these?" I answered in my Spirit– 'yea Lord. Thou knowest.'

I had come to the point where I realized that it was not the things of God that would satisfy but that it was God himself. After this insight came many words of love in my Spirit and I was revived. If one lacks understanding of his process then one can quit at the brink of victory. "Wisdom is the principal thing; therefore get wisdom: and with all your getting get understanding" (Proverbs 4:7). The Lord grants us understanding.

> "Wisdom is the principal thing; therefore get wisdom: and with all your getting get understanding" (Proverbs 4:7).

There are so many things in the World and in the experiences of the children of God to cause despair. However, if we understand the scripture and take the Lord at his word then we will overcome this wile. A personal relationship with the Lord and his Christ can be the difference between death and life. There is a lively message of hope, cling to this message and search for the hand of the Lord in every situation. For in so doing, you will spare yourself much pain of heart.

Final analysis

Everything in our lives is carefully positioned to work together for our good. Therefore whatever God has promised us will serve not only the purpose we suppose it should serve but it will be a multi- faceted package. For example, when God promised and placed me in a job, I thought it were only to be for time passing until I was ready for my next level in Him or rather for the purpose of financial gains to help me to get by. However, I found that it was way more than that. It happened to be to change the lives of many, to teach me lessons I otherwise would not have known and so many other things that I learnt as the days went by.

The promise that God made to Abraham was not just to make Him happy with a child but to show the mercies, grace and plans that God has for his people. This goes without saying that when God has made a promise to us, the time schedule given may be for your preparation and not for the delivering of the product. Therefore delay does not necessarily mean denial but it means that God is acting in his own- 'on time way'. One preacher said that some people are single because they did not ask God for any average mate. They asked God for the best and it takes time to process the best as well as to process you for the best.

In the times that we live, it is easy to feel despair and the enemy knows that if there is no hope then we will faint. We have a lively hope for though the natural things may not work to our benefit; we have an eternal hope that does not make us ashamed. The promises of God are yea and yea and he promised that He SHALL return to take us unto himself. This should be enough of a reason to hope and keep our eyes fixed on the prize. The very nature of hope requires that the object be absent. "For we are saved by hope: but hope that is seen is not hope: for what a man sees, why does he yet hope for?" (Romans 8:24). Therefore when the promise has not come to pass, it is not that God has forfeited, for there are no disappointments in God but rather that you have a reason to hope. The enemy places despair in the condition where hope should spring but it is up to us to view things from the correct perspective. We must hope in God.

> Therefore when the promise has not come to pass, it is not that God has forfeited, for there are no disappointments in God. It is rather that you have a reason to hope

Chapter seven

The wile of 'The Pride of Life'

Pride is a belief or an attitude in humans that they are not good enough until they can show that they are better than others. Pride seeks to compare itself with its neighbor and to compete with or belittles that one. Whereas envy is complacent and wishes for others to be the same, pride will work its life out to be the best thing around. The pride of life which I will henceforth refer to as pride is the love of things in this life that can show ones supremacy; whether it is education, money, possession or position. The word here used means, properly, ostentation or boasting, and then arrogance or pride. It refers to whatever there is that tends to promote pride, or that is an index of pride, such as the ostentatious display of dress, equipage, furniture, etc.

> Pride seeks to compare itself with its neighbour and to compete with or belittles others

The enemy uses this wile in a temporal way as well as in a Spiritual way. I will focus on the Spiritual pride. Among equals, pride is not readily seen but when there are a number of persons of different socio economic backgrounds then pride can raise its ugly head. There is no better place to find this mix than in our local churches. A place where school principals, teachers, dress makers, ancillary workers, garbage collectors, the housewives, lumbers jacks, Lawyers, entrepreneurs and all types of persons gather for worship. The Devil knows that he has to do whatever he can to prevent the church from being on one accord and of the same mind. We saw where unity caused God to come down from heaven to see what man was doing as they became one united force in building what was later called the tower of Babel. The enemy therefore knows that unity is strength. So he moves in and disrupts by infusing the Spirit of competitiveness through Pride.

Unity is strength

There is a tendency for those who enter the church as well established members in society to carry over that feeling of superiority into the place of worship. When they find out that others are equal to them on a Spiritual platform or even more anointed than they are then it poses a problem. This problem is heightened especially when the person who is ahead of them Spiritually is less educated than they are or less established in material things.

Another sore point is a situation in which those who have been in the church for many years find new comers who are out doing them in Spiritual operations. Some tend to get jealous and then a competition starts. A competition of which God who gives all Spiritual gifts would never be a part. This therefore causes people to testify lies, prophesy falsely, speak in Babel instead of a heavenly language and other such things. Pride breeds the Spirits of deception, lust, murder, envy, hatred, cruelty and jealousy. Let us look at all of these traits, evident in proud Satan himself.

Illustration

The Devil used the wile of 'the pride of Life' to get dominion over earth and attempted to get dominion over heaven also. It is one of his chief devices and first to be used on human beings. We can be sure that Satan is motivated by pride since his aim is to be better than God and he believes he will achieve this by hoarding as many people and things as is possible for his kingdom. Satan craves power and authority and so he is strengthened when someone else falls under his governance by yielding to his devices. Satan's aim was to take over heaven and the throne of God.

"How art thou fallen from heaven, O Lucifer, son of the morning! How art thou cut down to the ground, which didst weaken the nations! For thou hast said in thine heart, I will ascend into heaven, I will exalt our throne above the stars of God: I will sit also upon the mount of the congregation, in the sides of the north: I will ascend above the heights of the clouds; I will be like the most High. Yet thou shalt be brought down to hell, to the sides of the pit" (Isaiah 14:12-15).

However he was cast out without the opportunity to overthrow God. He was so arrogant and full of pride that he decided that he was going to seek for dominion over heaven and earth no matter how long it took or how much lying and deceiving he had to do.

> Pride is the earliest device used on the human race

Pride personified

Adam and Eve were created in an environment of utopia. According to an old preacher in his message *I'm glad I Repented*. "Everything was there in the garden when the man got there. However, the woman had it better because everything was there when she got there; including the man." God gave man dominion over all his creation.

"And God blessed them and God said unto them, be fruitful and multiply, and replenish the earth, subdue it: and have **dominion over** the fish of the sea, over the fowl of the air, and over every living thing that moveth upon the earth" (Genesis 1:28).

The man and woman were doing well until Adam allowed Eve by herself and she met the Devil. Now the enemy planted a seed in Eve's head that if she ate of the tree from which God had commanded her not to eat, then she would be like God- {A lie}. It was the pride of life in Eve that somehow liked the Devil's presentation of disobedience. So it was the pride in Satan that got into Eve through their interaction. Satan knew that "to whom we yield ourselves servants to obey, his servant we are…" (Roman 6:16). Also, when a man becomes a servant of another, the master gets dominion over the goods or property of that servant. Eve, being outside of the presence of God had no knowledge of such and neither did her husband. The Devil on the other hand knew full well what he was doing.

So Adam and Eve obeyed the Devil and hence gave him dominion over the earth. That is how Satan became "... The God of this world..." (II Corinthians 4:4). They also passed death to every mankind *{murder}*.

Now hundreds of years later, the Devil tried the same wile on the second Adam."...the first man is of the earth, earthly: the second man is the Lord from heaven" (I Corinthians 16:47). If we understand this, it can be seen that in acquiring dominion over earth through the first Adam becoming a servant to sin, the Devil could gain dominion over heaven if Christ obeyed him. Christ had all power in heaven "...all power in heaven is given unto me" (St. Matthew 28:18). In the very way that all dominion of earth was given to the first Adam as shown in Genesis 1:28, all dominion of heaven was in the second man Adam. Satan knew who Jesus was and this was later revealed in the Gospel of St. Mark 4:7 where the legions cried out "... what have I to do with thee, Jesus, thou son of the most high God?"

> The Devil could gain dominion over heaven
> if Christ obeyed him

This shows that when Satan approached Jesus in the wilderness and asked for worship, he was well aware of the implications of Jesus obeying this. Had Jesus obeyed then all power in Heaven would be given to Satan. But praise God, this was not done.

Practical application

What then is the pride of life and how is it applicable to you and me? The Pride of life refers to an over bearing hunger or desire for things of this life such as temporal knowledge, lavish clothing, furniture etc. for the sole reason of showing prestige over others.

Eve heard the idea of being wise like God and found it enticing. There are certain things she did not know. Like the fact that an increase in knowledge amounts to an increase in responsibility. Or that whatever God has prepared for us is better handled in the time for which God has ordained it.

> An increase in knowledge amounts to an increase in
> responsibility

Are you proud in Spirit? It will hinder your ability to function effectively. It will cause you to wander away from the plan of God for your life. The Bible says that "...God resisteth the proud, and giveth grace to the humble" (I Peter 5:5). If you are ashamed of the place where you worship because the building is not as palatial as other places of worship then you are proud. If you are unable to identify with the fact that you are equal to all the children of God where status in Christ is concerned then you are proud. If you do not attend services because you do not have a new suit, or you refuse to listen to a leader because he or she is younger than you are or less anointed then you suffer from pride. If you are quick to say you are humble then- you are filled with pride.

The hardest of all is this if you are unable to take instruction from those who are leading in a particular ministry of which you are a part because you know they had fallen and have risen again then you also suffer from pride. The truth is that human beings are very vulnerable to this wile. At one time or another each of us have had our encounter with pride; either when our anointing increased or when we got saved or when we got financial overflow. It has happened to you.

Part II

The root cause of Pride

If pride is so dangerous, why then do so many of us fall prey to it? Pride is a Spirit that comes to destroy the soul. It is of the flesh and we already know from the scriptures that "….the flesh warreth against the Spirit and the Spirit against the flesh" (Galatians 5:17). A Spirit cannot influence our actions until we give it a space in our thoughts. One preacher usually says that "the mind is like a fertile soil; once a thought drops in it and is watered, it flourishes". If we therefore allow the thoughts of the imps to find place in our hearts then we have already become captive to that Spirit. When a seed falls into the mind, and finds soil then it may seem to have disappeared but it is actually developing roots so that it can shoot. We can think of it as a seed thrown in an open well- watered field. Though we forget it, it will very well spring up and bear fruit.

It is so easy to become proud in a world that equips us to achieve all we can so that we can be better than those around us. We can be vulnerable to the Spirit of pride by the natural principles upon which the Kingdom operates. God gives gifts according to the grace that is given to us. This alone puts the flesh in trouble. We are apt to believe that the older and prettier and more educated would be treated better. This is not so with God but he rather to choose "…the weak things of the world to confound the things which are mighty" (I Corinthians 1:27).

Can you imagine your being in the kingdom for over 10 years being out performed by a new convert because of that person's level of gifting?

Room for pride you might say. But on the other hand, can you imagine your being a new convert and miracles and healing are being wrought through you. Greater room for pride.

> Because of the way the kingdom of God operates,
> there is great room for pride

The enemy knows our weak spots. He is aware of the human desire to be the best or rather better than others but it is for us to stifle and rather resist this urge. The kingdom is about each one bearing the other's burden and weeping with those who weep as well as laughing with those who laugh. One preacher said that if God has blessed my neighbor it means he is still in the blessing business and I may be next.

Part III

Erasing Pride

One morning as I worked on this chapter, the Lord woke me up with these words from Romans 12- "…mind not high things, but condescend to men of low estate…". This was also linked to the passage in Jeremiah 45 in which Baruch was worried as Jeremiah's ministry seemed to be crumbling. The Lord wanted Baruch to resist seeking power or a position because all flesh would be destroyed. The important thing was that he would escape with his life. If what we are seeking is of this life then moth and rust will destroy it. If also the sole reason is to be exalted among men then we need to shun it. In terms of Spiritual gifts there is also a way to deal with the possible pride that may accompany such.

"For who maketh thee to differ from another? and what hast thou that thou didst not receive? now if thou didst receive it, why dost thou glory, as if thou hadst not received it?" (I Corinthians 4:7). All that we have were received and so there is no room for boasting. I have seen what pride has done to many persons. It has wiped out the Christian faith of many and has left many Spiritually asleep. I will share one such case with you.

Anecdote

Our local home church in Jamaica was a small congregation of less than 100 members in the year 2008. Around the time when I started writing this book something quite relevant occurred. Pride took over one of our members.

A church brother had sinned against the church and so was openly punished by being asked to sit in an area which was designated for those being disciplined. He refused to do so and even told some persons that he would never obey such instruction from our Pastor. He continued in that same Spirit for months until he stopped attending church. I spoke to him on many occasions in an effort to bring him to the truth that he could never grow in God until he returned to church and served the time in the prescribed pew. Pride engulfed him so much that he went to another church and tried to acquire membership but could not do so without our pastor's written consent. He therefore started to visit other churches in our area but never tried to pay his due.

He returned to church one particular Sunday and I spoke with him again. This time he acknowledged that what I was saying was indeed true and so he said that he was ready to serve his time. He spoke to Pastor briefly and made an agreement. I however noticed that he did not sit in the designated area that Sunday so I was somewhat puzzled. He did not come back to church for a while either and I did not hear much about him. I then got wind of information that he was about to start a new movement. He even spoke openly about and against our pastor.

A few weeks later, a preacher visited our church from Canada. The same preacher who had confirmed my mandate to write this book was the one used by God. On the same day that he prophesied to me he prophesied the young fellow's doom. It was prophesied that somebody was working against our Pastor's ministry and that he would surely die. Not many days after this prophecy, this once fervent brother lost his job, failed to launch his movement and ran away from our part of town.

It is clear that this young man was held in bondage by the Spirit of pride; he was defenseless. He had allowed the Spirit of Pride to take control of his life as those described in II Timothy 2:26- "And that they may recover themselves out of the snare of the Devil, who are taken captive by him at his will". He chose himself over salvation. As I write these lines it comes to mind that I could have prayed for him and bind the Spirit of pride. Now the thought also comes that even then, he could not be freed unless he recognized his problem and acknowledged his need for help. Pride is a Spirit that will overtake whosoever will.

> Pride over takes whosoever will

In Practice

You can Curse and resist this evil Spirit of pride and it will go. We are not servants of sin and so we can resist the Devil and he must flee. I experienced this one Sunday in church. I had to bind the Spirit of covetousness and jealousy which are both off springs of pride. As I sat in church one Sunday morning having just entered into a period of Praise, I watch a much older brethren than myself leading and suddenly I got jealous. The red flag in my conscience went up and I responded immediately. I said "the blood of Jesus is against you Spirit of jealousy and coveteousness". I said "I bind you in the name of Jesus." I then spoke to my mind so I could redirect it to praising and the Devil slowly went.

> Resist the Devil and he will flee from you

Explained

Pride is a flesh serving emotion. We therefore know that it automatically works against the Spirit since the Galatians writer said in 5:17 "For the flesh lusts against the Spirit, and the Spirit against the flesh: and these are contrary the one to the other: so that you cannot do the things that you would". When we glory in the flesh and please our sinful nature, we displease God and so our Spirit suffers. Therefore to hurt and damage the sinful nature called the flesh, we need to act contrary to it. So then, if the flesh is telling you to be jealous over someone else's success then you just need to feed it with a scripture like: rejoice with them that rejoice. Not only should you feed it with the scripture but you need also to do the action and stop jealousy in its tracks.

> Counteract your struggle with a scripture

There is a very powerful lesson which I have learnt over the first year of writing this book. This is the revelation that if I allow sin a small place in my heart then it will become harder to get rid of as it matures in me.

Anecdote

I had a situation where I was displeased about the actions of a kingdom citizen. I thought about what that individual had done until it started to mature into hatred. I realized this and yet I did not stop it until it was out of my control. I was held bound by a Spirit of hatred. I had to cry out to God and surrender myself to Him totally for him to release me and that is how I got away. I almost lost my salvation had it not been for grace. We therefore need to stop pride in its track. We need to prevent it from gaining access because once it gains entrance into our hearts, it spreads like wild fire. It is like a little fox that can spoil the vine.

> Pride is a little fox that can spoil the vine

Explained

When one is lifted up in pride, he or she will see all others as below him or herself. One way to keep the Spirit of pride away is by seeking for as many opportunities as possible in which to serve. When we serve, we deny flesh and directly obey the command of Jesus Christ to serve each other. We also operate the way Jesus did as he washed his disciples' feet. Tasks in the church that seem menial are there so that we can keep our flesh under subjection and keep the Spirit of pride away.

> Menial tasks are meant to humble us

When the Spirit of pride attacks you then remember this: a Spirit does not remain in an area where it is not being fed because that will make it weak. This is why when Satan is resisted he flees because as you resist him his control weakens over your life. Therefore gird up the loins of your mind and be sober. For God has not given you a Spirit of fear but of a sound mind.

Seeing then that if we allow pride in, it will take root and enslave us then we are to resist same. We were bound but are now made free through the blood of Jesus; therefore let us not be not entangled again in the yoke of bondage.

If we shod our feet with preparation of the gospel of peace then whatever seems to cause division or strife we will walk away from it. Pride is one such culprit that we need to leave behind.

> God resiseth the PROUD but giveth more grace
> to the HUMBLE

Chapter eight

The wile of DISUNITY

While some people, like our Lord Jesus, are readily lovable, others, who are in the process (which is the majority) pose a very serious challenge to us. However, love is not defined by the attitude of the loved but by the character of the lover. The scriptures say "Herein is love, not that we loved God, but that he loved us, and sent his Son to be the propitiation for our sins" (I John 4:10). It is not such a big deal that we love a perfect God but that he loves an imperfect us. As a matter of fact we were his enemies for the scripture also says in Romans 5:8 "But God commends his love toward us, in that, while we were yet sinners, Christ died for us." There is nothing in us that deserved the love of God so it was accounted a gift.

> People in the process are difficult to love but we are all in the process

The Process

When the Lord called us, he called raw material that was to be processed unto perfection. He gave us of his Spirit which works upon our lives area by area. Being unique creatures, no two persons have identical flaws or character. Therefore the work of God in me would be unique to me. Many times because we have been perfected in a particular area of our lives we expect others to also be at that level which is rarely ever so. We tend to despise those who display faults which we find unbearable without even realizing that we were once the same before the Lord changed us. One thing I have learnt is that the Lord often allows our faults with which we are comfortable to hurt us into realizing that we need to change. Therefore, sometimes the people we despise are often simply being processed in this way. The love of God which we profess to have, loves through the process unto perfection.

> The love of God loves us through   the process

If then the love of God is in us, that love which looks beyond faults, then we should also love the brethren whom God himself loves. Love operates in such a way that even if the object does not deserve kindness, it is afforded such. So much so that while we were yet his enemies Christ died for us. We therefore must love our enemies as Christ loves us.

> God loves the World which includes all enemies

Hence, there should be no room for disunity among the people of God. It is understandable that the wolf and the sheep will not thrive well together because the former would always be trying to devour the latter. But the people of God whom God loves and died for should be able to live in unity. As a matter of fact God so loved the WORLD. "Beloved, if God so loved us, we ought also to love one another" (I John 4:11).

Disunity or discord is a Spirit that the enemy has used for decades in an attempt to cripple the work of God among his people. It is widely known what Jesus said "…every kingdom divided against itself is brought to desolation; and every city or house divided against itself shall not stand:" (St. Matthew 12:25). It is also known that a people who are united are a force to be reckoned with. They are an almost invincible army that has limitless potential. The people of God so often shun or overlook this truth. Let us analyze it.

> A house divided against itself must fall

Illustrated

The first place in the scriptures where we see total unity is in the story of the tower of Babel (Genesis 11). The people got so united in their thrust that the Lord had to come down to see what they were doing. A united effort draws God's attention that he leaves his holy habitation. When the Lord realized that the people could do almost anything they set their minds to, he had to scatter them abroad.

> A united people can do whatever they put their minds to

Explained

"'These six things does the LORD hate: yes, seven are an abomination to him: a proud look, a lying tongue, and hands that shed innocent blood, an heart that devises wicked imaginations, feet that be swift in running to mischief, a false witness that speaks lies, and he that sows discord among brothers" (Proverbs 6:16-19).

There are persons in the local church who they themselves get along with almost everyone. They also mingle and fellowship with both good and evil. In so doing, they do all that is humanly possible to cause division. They do this by carrying falsehood and by fuelling every offence made. They do this in ignorance of the scripture which clearly state in Proverbs 17:9 "He that covers a transgression seeks love; but he that repeats a matter separates very friends."

However they keep doing terrible things to their utter destruction.

> God hates one who causes discord among brethren

A divided Church is like a house that is being built in which as one person lays a block while another person immediately uses a sledge hammer to dislocate the laid block.

Analogy

Just as I edited this chapter I was in a convocation under the theme 'Rebuilding the altar, reclaiming the power'. This theme is so appropriate for this chapter since the altar refers to foundational teachings and principles. The most fundamental principle of Christianity is unity. For, as the disciples waited in the upper room on one accord, the Holy Ghost fell upon them. The people of God must be united to rebuild the things that were once removed so that the power of God can operate freely in the church.

Part II

Why are we so vulnerable to the Spirit of disunity?

We are vulnerable to any wile because we lack crucial parts of the armour of God. If we had on the breastplate of righteousness then our hearts would desire to do what is right. This wile of disunity is fueled by a lack of love among the people of God but there are still deeper roots than just this.

> We are vulnerable to any wile when we lack crucial parts of the armour of God

Unmerciful

A mark of the last day's generation would be that they are unmerciful. This Spirit is very evident in the world and it has indeed spilled over into the church. It is very easy for us humans to be divided. This is so because we tend to prefer not to relate to persons who oppose our views and opinion on things. Persons who disturb our order are usually tabooed and ostracized. It is even easier for us in church to fall prey to disunity. This is so because once a person seems to be transgressing God's law, then despite the fact that we ourselves also fall at times, we tend to label them as goats or waywards. Goats or wolves they are usually called and we are eager to set these people aside. It then becomes scriptural according to us that these should be alienated.

89

We then move towards getting others to rally around us in our bid to 'save' them from the 'wolf'. Due to the fact that everyone has a circle, the so labeled wolf and his team, along with the instigator, cause a crack. If cracks are not fixed they tend to break out into a huge chasm.

> If cracks are not fixed they will cause a huge chasm

Disobedience

Another reason we fall so easy to this wile of disunity is because we do not follow the scriptures. The instructions of God are very humbling and so if followed they can both change our lives and the lives of the haters or oppressors. We often act through impulse and cause hurt or even greater damage than would otherwise have been done.

The scripture bids us to warn them that are unruly. We are at no time told that once a person transgresses then that means the person is a goat or that he has lost sonship. Though the writer of first John says that he who sins is of the Devil, he is referring to those who willfully sin and not all who fall into sin. We therefore are not expected to pronounce a verdict immediately as there is a falling to condemn someone into leading life away from the children of God. The scripture actually gives us the guidelines to follow when a brother or sister transgresses. This is clearly outlined in St. Matthew 18.

> We must obey the scripture in its entirety

According to the mentioned scripture, we should first confront the person, and then if the person continues we should bring a witness. After that, we should take them to the church and if they still do not adjust then we should put them aside until they change or express the need for help to do so. Nowhere are we told to spread the news to all brethren when a brother or sister is transgressing and neither are we instructed to ostracize them before following the three- step procedure.

The real reason we are so vulnerable is because we are naturally selfish creatures. Some of us lack the love of God and so when we meet upon anyone who falls short we refuse to show mercy. Did you know that some brethren do not confront other brethren with faults because they want them to feel the wrath of God? Such cruelty should not be among the people of God.

False teachers

Some saints have been crippled by false teaching. This causes a divide in the house of the Lord. Sometimes these differences in belief cause a rift that seems impossible to mend. No one is willing to let go of his belief or even to admit that he may be wrong. Therefore, after a while there is a level of uncertainty about who Is saved and who is not since such controversies usually breed the thought that somebody must be wrong and out of tune with God.

Unforgiveness

Even in the house of the Lord some people suffer hurt at the hands of their brethren. These hurts can be so bad at times that one refuses to let go the injury. This type of attitude causes one to be bitter and revengeful. This can go on for months and years until there is a great divide.

Lack of understanding

Each Christian is at his own level of maturity in Christ. The babes will do things that are not becoming of the matured believer. If there is a lack of understanding then the more matured may tend to ostracize the weaker ones instead of strengthening them with the Word of God.

There is also a lack of understanding that unity is strength and that a house divided against itself must fall. If this were understood then all who mean well in the Kingdom of God would do that which is in their power to bring unity to the church.

> Understanding is of the essence

Favouritism

There is yet another demon that causes Disunity in the house of the Lord; that of Favouritism. The scripture speaks clearly in the book of James about this topic. It says that we must use fairness and equity in dealing with people. However, the people of God sometimes waste time in exalting one leader over another even though promotion comes from God. Some even go as far as to boycott the ministry of one leader because they do not like him or her and build up a divide in the house of God. These people are not without their reward.

> Promotion comes from God so who are we to discriminate?

Part III

How then do we kill the wile of disunity?

The remedy for disunity is the love of God. Since we are admonished not only to love the Lord and ourselves but also to love our brethren and our enemies, then love has to be the answer. The love of God is the love that loves in spite of. When we receive Christ he enlarges our capacity to love. The love of God is such that it looks for a point of restoration. It looks for an occasion to do good. It loves us into changing; Loves us and pursues us when we err.

> The remedy for disunity is love

As earlier said, ''People in the process'' will make mistakes and because we are all in the process together, whatever causes one person to stumble could also cause us to stumbled. For this cause we should not criticize but rather exhort, so that we can save a soul from hell. Some people revel in other people's displeasure and so when one transgresses the command of God, instead of restoring in quietness, that person may seek to ensure that it is well published. The very thought of this displeases God. What we are to do is to seek out the person and help to bring him back to his feet.

Did you know that God looks for an intercessor who will plead for mercy on our behalf whenever we are straying? Did you know that he keeps his eyes on us even when we are leaving him and are out of his fold? Paul was so confident that he asked what could separate him from the love of God in Romans 8.

> God provides us an intercessor when we are straying so that he has a reason to spare us

If we then can become like God what then can separate us from loving our brethren? The apostle Paul admonishes us to be transformed by the renewing of our minds. The easiest thing to do is to encourage the person to make the changes if he is failing. Then there is something more powerful that we can do.

Expounded

We have 'speaking rights' in the kingdom of God. "Death and life are in the power of the tongue…" (Proverbs 18:21). It is said in the book of Job that we shall declare a thing and it shall come to pass. We also wrestle not against flesh and blood but against principalities and powers. Therefore when the Spirit of disunity rises for whatever reason we can tear it down completely. When we counter this Spirit then the rest becomes easy. This is so because this Spirit of disunity blocks our desire to do good. Once that Spirit is crushed then it is time to attack the cause of the disunity which may very well be another tearing down procedure. Whenever one Spirit has to be evicted it is likely that others are also present there or lingering nearby to gain occupancy.

If you are wondering how we war against these Spirit then it is simple. We acknowledge the power of God then speak to the Spirit and bind it then command it to leave. The questions is asked- how can a man spoil a strong man's house? The answer is that "…first bind the strong man? and then he will spoil his house" (Matthew 12:29).

> We can speak things into being and they must obey us

In this very way, if someone hurts us and we cannot seem to be healed then we can speak to our hearts and healing must take place. There is nothing impossible to them that believe.

Illustrated

One evening as I was at home, I had a very disturbing conversation with a brethren in the Lord. The person was emotionally distraught. It was so terrible that things seemed hopeless even to the most positive mind. The Spirit directed me to do something. I then went down in prayer. I focused and went up in the Spirit, positioned myself in the person's environs, took authority over the atmosphere then stood in the gap and spoke order and normalcy. A few hours later when I next spoke to the brethren, things were more than normal. Things were going very well.

We can do the same for all situations that seem to be causing or has the potential to cause disunity. We just need to be sensitive to the voice of God, be obedient to his voice then be willing to do whatever he says to do. We can win all the time by saying nothing to a human but taking all these Spiritual situations to the Spiritual platform because the anointing makes the difference.

> All battles are fought in the Spirit

Anecdote

I came upon a conflict in the House of the Lord that seemed to have had the potential for a great divide. This conflict was among the leadership of the house. Some leaders believed one thing while another set believed another. As I tried to make sense of such a difference in belief the Lord brought a situation to my attention. He ministered to me the situation between Paul and Peter. In the earlier part of his ministry, Peter believed strictly that salvation was only of the Jews while Paul had gotten the mandate to preach to the Gentiles. There was a common ground. Both men desired and were equipped and instructed by God to preach. Therefore, to prevent a split in the early church, they decided that Peter would be the Apostle to the Jews and Paul would be the Apostle to the Gentiles; just as the Lord had willed. This caused much soothing in that early church's problem and so it did in my church.

> We must fervently work to find common grounds

Many times, issues of conflict simply need a compromise or a common point. No matter how persons are fuming and have established two sides, there is always some common ground. Let us look for the common ground and let the work of God go on. If we are finding it difficult to love someone then there is a solution given by God. Pray for such a one and you will definitely start loving him.

> Praying for those who are difficult to love makes us love them greatly

Disunity does not help the church of God. What it does is it pushes people away from the kingdom and enlarges the kingdom of the Devil. It is only through unity that we will find strength to do great exploits for God. "And above all things have fervent charity among yourselves: for charity shall cover the multitude of sins" (I Peter 4:8).

> United we stand but divided we fall

Chapter nine

The wile

Repeated

I was not even very sure about what to call this, the concluding chapter. But there is a wile that the enemy uses. Let us call it the wile repeated. This refers to the wile that the enemy uses so often on us and usually gets the same reaction from us each time. This wile is unique for every individual because it is custom made. It is so built that it derails the individual every single time. It most naturally would be one of the eight previously discussed wiles or, an offspring thereof. This type of wile is closely connected to ones emotional nature. This wile is so effective because the enemy spends time to study our actions or reactions when orchestrating an attack with this wile. Once the wile produces a favourable result on one or two occasions then it becomes a key in the enemy's hand. He will then throw it at us as often as he can. Let me explain by example.

Anecdote

I had a friend for some years who the enemy just knew how to manipulate. He knew that once he got her to become insecure about her life's situations then she would shut down her Spiritual drive towards God. Therefore whenever she was at the brink of a Spiritual overflow then the Devil would attack her. For a number of years this went on without interruption until she decided that enough was enough.

I too had a similar conflict. I realized only after this thing had happened to me on about three occasions. I got to my senses and realized that whenever someone was not living right and I knew about it and felt that nothing was being done about it, I would get bitter against that one. It is known that bitterness clogs the Spirit and prevents a free flow between you and God. So I was walking into this block over and over again. For, sure enough, there were a few people who were always playing church. One evening as the enemy tried it again I stood up in the Holy Spirit and spoke against this evil Spirit binding it and declaring that I was not going to be affected negatively again. Things were different from then on.

Such an emotional conflict can occur in more areas than one. It is so effective because when we get emotional our rational thoughts get side lined and our judgment becomes impaired. By the time these emotions subside, the damage is usually so far done that we are left to do damage control on a bruised conscience.

Proper perspective

If the enemy gets to us with the wiles previously discussed then their off springs complete the work in us. Take for example the wile of despair. It is so designed to frustrate the child of God so that a worldly lifestyle looks greener. Once despair has done its perfect work then the wile of deception comes into play; Deception that the world is much more attractive than the congregation of the Lord. The enemy strings these wiles together to wipe out the saint completely. Therefore if we can kill the root of the wile then the offspring cannot harm us.

Of course the enemy does not quit using a wile at us simply because we have identified it. He moves back and mixes it with some other wile and attacks us again. The battle is never ending. Matthew tells us well when the explanation was being given about a man who was delivered from demon possession. The Lord said that when the demon returns and finds the man empty, swept and garnished, he returns and takes seven other Spirits with himself and enters in.

Final analysis

The enemy of the Lord will always be the enemy of his children. There is an ongoing war in the cosmos that will rage unto the great battle of Armageddon. Until then it is for us the children of God to put on the whole armour of God that we may be able to quench the fiery darts of the enemy. The Word of God is always a good weapon to have stored in our hearts because it is the sword of the Spirit. Let us therefore live for the Lord and be watchful for the enemy who is the devourer that comes only to steal, kill and destroy that which he has not labored to plant.

We have the weapons to win and we shall win because greater is he that is in us than he that is in the world. Also, when the enemy comes upon us like a flood then the Lord will raise up a standard in us. It is known that the battle is not ours but it is the Lord's. We are very confident also that the Lord is with us always, even unto the end of the world.

Most importantly we are assured that it is not by might, nor by power but it is by my Spirit, SAITH THE LORD. It is a Spirit work.

KEEP ON THE FIRING LINE.

Better is on before us
